MARKETING MATTERS

For Small & Medium Enterprises:

Now More Than Ever!

MARKETING MATTERS

For Small & Medium Enterprises:
Now More Than Ever!

Alan C. Middleton PhD

First edition, 2022

Publisher: American Marketing Association, Toronto Chapter

Cover & interior layout design by Andy Meaden meadencreative.com

Copy Editor: Miglena Nikolova

Middleton, Alan. C. Marketing Matters: Now More than Ever! / Alan C. Middleton, PhD

p. cm. Originally published with sponsorship of American Marketing Association Toronto Chapter, 2022.

ISBN Paperback 978-1-7778-0662-0

ISBN eBook 978-1-7778-0663-7

CONTENTS

FOREWORD

As a marketing professional, a business leader and someone that has scaled a business in Canada and ultimately taken that business around the globe, I have had the opportunity to work with many of Canada's largest companies as well as a number of small and medium sized enterprises. Working alongside these organizations, I always appreciated the dedication of the leadership teams and their drive to succeed but I also often found myself in discussions around whether they were fully invested in their approach to marketing. So imagine the smile on my face when Alan Middleton approaches me to write the Foreward to his new book that is focused on "why marketing matters, now more than ever".

Alan and I have a shared experience that doesn't completely overlap but is full of enough professional marketing parallels that we have a common view on many marketing, business and leadership related topics. We even share a few industry awards as two years ago, after a long career in marketing, I was inducted into the AMA's Marketing Hall of Legends, a mere sixteen years after Alan Middleton was recognized with the same honour. But as I reviewed this book and reflected on our conversations, respective careers and experiences, I reaffirmed that we have a lot more in common than industry recognition. We both believe that a discipline of great, thoughtful marketing plays a vital role in the success of a company or organization. We share a passion for helping our partners to succeed and know that putting the customer at the centre of an organizations purpose is a critical part of that journey. And finally, we understand the value of inspiring a team to fully adopt a marketing strategy in a way that brings your brand and customer experience to life.

I also believe that there is no denying the two fundamental premises that Middleton puts forward in his most recent book. First, Canada's growth is dependent on the success of the many small and medium sized enterprises that make up the vast majority of our economy. Second, marketing is a powerful and foundational tool for SME's looking to leverage the full power of a well thought out business strategy to drive their results. Canada's long-term potential is dependent on our ability to not only establish new SME's but also to be inspired as leaders to seek ways to fully realize their potential and keep those businesses in Canada, even as they spread their wings internationally. As Middleton points out in the book, we are often too quick to monetize early success by selling out to bigger international players when many of our SME's could be the next Shopify if we focused on the right strategies.

Central to achieving this goal (beyond financing and building a talented team) is the creation of an exceptional marketing plan and commitment to appropriately fund and execute against that plan. These elements are foundational to the successful execution of any marketing plan and it is from this framework that Middleton seeks to inspire Canadian leaders. What we experience as a reader is that Middleton has created a structured and insightful approach which is highly practical. It provides the reader with simple ways to assess where they are today and provides a series of questions that help identify their opportunities, clarify their intent and then build out a comprehensive marketing strategy for their business.

Bryan Pearson
Advisor, Board member, previous President/CEO Loyalty One

PREFACE

"I have not failed. I've just found 10,000 ways that won't work."

Thomas Edison, 1847 – 1931. American inventor and businessperson.

"Nobody talks about entrepreneurship as survival, but that is exactly what it is, and what it nurtures – creative thinking. Running that first shop taught me business is not financial science, it's about trading, buying and selling."

Anita Roddick, 1942 – 2007. British, founder of the Body Shop.

The Toronto chapter of the American Marketing Association is a leading chapter in North America and a leader in marketing training and development in Canada. Throughout its activities, entrepreneurship has been an important focus. Whether the enterprise is micro, small or medium size, or has grown to become a large organization, marketing is a key skill in achieving success.

This book recognizes that all too often, Canadian Small & Medium sized Enterprises (SMEs) undervalue the importance of full and ongoing marketing activity. The data you will see in this book confirms this.

This book also recognizes that all too often Canadian entrepreneurs think marketing is just communications – advertising/social media. While important, this is just one part of a good marketing approach. Here's how one author, Frederick Crane in his book "Marketing for Entrepreneurs", defines marketing:

"Marketing is the activity, set of institutions, and processes for creating, communicating, delivering, and exchanging offerings that have value for customers, clients, partners, and society at large."

The point is that great successful enterprises succeed by delivering value to customers, such that as Crane says:

"The actual purpose of an enterprise is the creation and retention of satisfied customers."

This short text draws on personal experience and current literature and thinking about marketing in micro, small & medium sized enterprises (SMEs). There are longer and more detailed books and articles referred to in the bibliography. What is important in this book are the cases of successful – and sometimes unsuccessful – marketing activities taken by entrepreneurs. In these, I have been privileged to draw on AMA Toronto Marketing Hall of Legends inductees who have been or are entrepreneurs. Over the last two decades it has been an impressive list:

Organization	Inductee(s)
Angus Reid (market research)	Angus Reid
Balmoral Multicultural Marketing agency	Sharifa Khan
Bensimon Byrne (advertising agency)	Jack Bensimon
Blackberry	Jim Balsillie
Canada Goose	Dani Reiss
Capital C (communications agency)	Tony Chapman
Cirque du Soleil	Guy Laliberté
Club Monaco	Joseph Mimran
Cossette Communications	Francois Duffar and Claude Lessard
D.W. & partners (design agency)	Don Watt
Dragons' Den panelist (TV show)	Arlene Dickinson
Four Season Hotels	Isadore ("Issy") Sharp
1-800-GOT-JUNK	Brian Scudamore
Harry Rosen	Harry Rosen
Honest Ed	Ed Mirvish
ING Direct	Arkadi Kuhlman
Jean Coutu	Jean Coutu
John Street (advertising agency)	Arthur Fleischmann
Kessler Productions (music production)	Syd Kessler
Level 5 (brand consultancy)	David Kincaid
Lise Watier Cosmetics	Lise Watier
Lowe Roche (advertising agency)	Geoffrey Roche
Loyalty One	Bryan Pearson
Lululemon	Chip Wilson
Mark Anthony Group (winery)	Anthony von Mandl
Nature's Path	Ratana and Arran Stephens

Padulo Inc. (advertising agency)	Rick Padulo
Roots Canada.	Michael Budman and Don Green
Saffer Retail	Morris Saffer
Shoppers Drug Mart	David Bloom and Murray Koffler
Signal Hill Equity Partners	Colleen Moorehead
Sleep Country Canada.	Stephen Gunn and Christine Magee
Taxi (advertising agency)	Paul Lavoie
Tim Hortons	Ron Joyce
Rogers Communications	Ted Rogers
Umbra	Les Mandelbaum and Paul Rowan
W.K. Buckley ("Buckley's")	Frank Buckley
WestJet Airlines	Clive Beddoe

Four of these are included in the SME Stories I have used to illustrate how SMEs learn and thrive. I have also included seven other micro, small and medium size SME stories. These also cover gender and geographic examples – no not absolutely everyone, but a number, to show the learning and how some of the SME marketing principles (and principals) work.

In addition to the worthy entrepreneurs listed above, a big thank you goes out to the AMA Toronto Board and its Advisory Council. A big thank you to:

The AMA Toronto 2021/22 President Tina Portillo

The endless support, work and friendship of Craig Lund, AMA Toronto Board Secretary and VP Membership and AMA Volunteer of the Year 2022; and Miglena Nikolova, Board

Member and previous President AMA Toronto who led the chapter to winning its first Silver Chapter of the Year award and recognition for its Diversity, Equity and Inclusion among over 70 chapters of the American Marketing Association.

Alan Middleton
May 15th 2022.

INTRODUCTION

"Marketing has been seen as one of the greatest problems faced by small and medium enterprises (SMEs), but simultaneously one of the most important activities for growth and survival."

Franco, de Fatima Santos, Ramalho and Nunes in "Journal of Small Business and Enterprise Development", May 2014.

The roughly 1.2 million Canadian SMEs represent the backbone of the Canadian economy in its employment, productivity, output, innovation and wealth created. As Canadians we often think and read about our major industries both domestically and foreign owned such as financial services, resources and transportation as primarily large enterprises. While there are large organizations (there were 12 Canadian owned organizations in the 2022 Fortune Global 500 list), the support to these and primary providers in the Canadian economy are SMEs. These Small businesses (1-99 employees) and Medium size businesses (100 – 500 employees) during 2012-2016 period accounted for about 51% of national Gross Domestic Product (GDP) for goods and 55% for services. In terms of goods exported, SMEs accounted for about 42% of total with the US being the dominant destination usually accounting for about 75% of merchandise exports with China, the UK, Japan, Mexico and Germany accounting for between 4% and 1% each.

With all the changes wrought by technology and the working and consumption changes accelerated by the pandemic, the challenges for SMEs in the Canadian economy are myriad. As Canadians, we need our SMEs to succeed and to scale up to achieve success for themselves, their communities and the country. This requires attention to 10 strategic principles:

- a business idea and strategy that delivers a business concept unique or better than competitors.

- an ambitious view and plan of the scale and the scope the enterprise could achieve.

- executed in a way that delivers consistent value and satisfaction for its customers.

- that delivers a positive working culture for its staff that encourages commitment, cooperation and innovation avoiding unnecessarily bureaucratic procedures.

- a development and succession plan for key managerial levels.

- a business model that manages pricing and costs profitably over time.

- a risk management strategy that fits the market it competes in and the resources available.

- sustainable use of natural and human resources.

- sufficient financial resources to enable establishment, growth, and expansion of the enterprise to achieve ongoing profit from its business concept.

- with the strategic ability, organizational flexibility and resources to enable changes and adjustments to organizational direction in the ever more competitive world of Volatility, Uncertainty, Complexity, Ambiguity (VUCA).

In addition to entrepreneurial drive and ambition, skills in appropriate technologies, accounting and finance and leadership and management, skills in marketing in the modern age are required.

There is evidence that of the challenges that Canadian SMEs face, three are of major significance:

- Sufficient and sustainable financing from varying sources: financial institutions, venture and angel investors, government grants, person-to-person.

- Engaging the appropriate quality of management personnel especially at the scale-up stage of SME development.

- The commitment and action to execute and fund sufficient and well- targeted activity in marketing.

This brief book focuses on the last issue. Canadian SMEs all too often underinvest in, and misunderstand, the importance of marketing in building a successful enterprise.

So, how to achieve improvement? What elements need to be considered?

Back in my business school days I would talk about the 5 Ps in the mix of marketing activity and how these need to be integrated in enterprise planning and execution:

- Product or service that is developed and sold.

- Place or distribution channels through which the product/service is sold and delivered.

- Price that is charged to the target group for use or purchase of the product/service.

- Promotion that informs and encourages the target group to become aware of, try and keep using the product/service.

- People and service: the staff who work in the enterprise, serve the target group and ensure high levels of customer satisfaction.

Some authors, such as David James Hood in his book *"Competitive SME"*, have recently talked about 16 Ps! They added many that I do consider valid. Here are 5 of them that I consider a priority:

- Project Management to be sure different tasks/organizational silos are well integrated.

- Priority which outlines the most important issues/actions on which to focus and in what order.

- Positioning: how the brand that represents the offering of the enterprise should be viewed by the target group in comparison with competition.

- Profit which focuses on how to achieve required net cash flow or funding.

- Pivot which outlines the ability of the organization to shift direction to promising new markets for the brand.

While the others are important, I would argue they need to be considerations within these ten, and that these <u>Marketing Mix 10 Ps</u> hold the core issues in achieving a competitive marketing mix. These are described in greater detail in the following chapters: **SME Marketing Challenge # 1 – 8.**

With few exceptions, Canadian SME history indicates we have an SME culture that is successful at innovation and new ideas yet does not want to tell potential customers about the resulting products/services. This is especially true compared to the US. On average, though varying by market sector, spending on just one measure of marketing activity, advertising, in the US Business-to-Consumer (B2C) businesses spend between 5 – 10% of sales revenues; on Business-to-Business (B2B) enterprises between 2 – 5% of sales revenues. The limited data on Canadian enterprises indicates the equivalent ratios are less than half of those!

Too many Canadian SMEs fail to achieve the promise of their product/service insights as they fail to tell sufficient customers about their products and services or build a brand that enables sufficient competitive protection.

In essence, Canadian SMEs develop great products and services but often don't effectively tell its value through its pricing, distribution availability or communication.

This then will be the underlying theme of the next chapters. I will examine this theme in a way that is not intended to criticize, but to be helpful to SMEs. The theme will be tackled under the following headings:

- SME Marketing Challenge #1 – Target Group: Customer and Potential Customer Knowledge (identifying and really getting to know and understand your target market, benefits sought, and how they see competition).

- SME Marketing Challenge #2 – Building your Sustainable Brand (marketing is not just advertising, how to build your primary marketing asset, a strong brand).

- SME Marketing Challenge #3 – Develop and Staff a Strategic and Operational Marketing Plan.

- SME Marketing Challenge #4 – Communicate, communicate, communicate.

- SME Marketing Challenge #5 – Staff and customers are 'two sides of the same coin'.

- SME Marketing Challenge #6 – Building your international business.

- SME Marketing Challenge #7 – Scaling Up – lessons in executive marketing management.

- SME Marketing Challenge #8 – Concluding thoughts.

Within these chapters we will cover topics like essential marketing principles, classic marketing mistakes, the crossover between sales and digital and non-digital marketing communications, and the importance of marketing in growing an enterprise.

In addition, each chapter will include a format for planning and thinking about the topic. Termed **SME Marketing Challenge Tools**, these should help develop a disciplined but non-bureaucratic approach to the issues.

First, though, a viewpoint.

Marketing is not just an executional process; it is a high-level business strategy. Marketing develops sales but is not sales: sales and marketing activities are two sides of the same coin. Marketing has both short-term goals: getting customers to buy now; and longer-term brand building goals, i.e. getting customers to understand, buy and repeat use of your brand. A strong brand is a major financial asset for an organization and as such is a primary goal of marketing and a critical business objective. Marketing is a strategic and operational interaction between identifying the best target customers, planning your product/service offering(s), pricing it, determining the best channels of distribution (direct or via agents, retailers, or others), promoting it through advertising and promotion activity (digital and non-digital) and importantly having the best organized, motivated and trained staff serving the customer and providing improvements.

All these areas are more important than ever in the post-pandemic world where an ever-increasing number of national and international competitors are fighting for the business and the trust of customers.

Also included as part of the chapters are eleven **SME Stories.** These are the stories around successful SMEs – from micro to medium in size and those who have grown further, who have used marketing most successfully in their development. These stories indicate their progress and learning as enterprises and hopefully, stimulate readers to apply these thoughts and learning in their own enterprises. The first is a story of a small enterprise, but first let's define what the Marketing Mix is and the elements that need attending to:

SME Marketing Challenge Intro.
Tool: The Marketing Mix 10 Ps:

1. <u>Product or service</u> that is developed and sold and how it will be updated and deliver a real benefit versus competition.

2. <u>Place or distribution channels</u> through which the product/service is sold and delivered and how these can provide an integrated option for the target group so that they can acquire it quickly, conveniently, safely and in the best condition.

3. <u>Price</u> that is charged to the target group for use or purchase of the product/service. Additionally, any discount guidelines to ensure the brand 'on deal' percentage does not become excessive and result in a perceived price cut and reduction in the value. Contemporary AI based price optimization systems enable modeling based on price elasticities.

4. <u>Promotion: marketing communications</u> that informs and encourages the target group to become aware of, try and keep using the product/service. It is critical to develop a Marketing Communications mix of advertising, social media, web site and sampling and other promotions that are consistent yet fit the target group's life and is affordable.

5. <u>People and service</u>: the staff who work in the enterprise, deal with the target group and ensure high levels of customer satisfaction. These days this is critical as skilled and motivated employees are key to enterprise success.

6. <u>Project Management</u> to be sure different tasks/organizational silos are well integrated. Marketing has many elements, often these are handled by different people. The process must be integrated.

7. <u>Priority</u> which outlines the most important issues/actions on which to focus and in what order. Remember that sometimes what seems urgent may not be as important as something less urgent. Priorities should recognize progress towards important goals.

8. <u>Positioning</u>: how the brand that represents the offering of the enterprise should be viewed by the target group in comparison with competition. This will be discussed in the chapter on branding.

9. <u>Profit</u> which focuses on how to achieve required net cash flow or funding. A key issue here is to remember that profit comes not only from revenue but also expense management. Profit improvement can come from reviewing both revenue and cost areas. But, caution! As indicated in earlier sections there is a tendency for Canadian SMEs to underinvest in Marketing Communications (MarCom.).

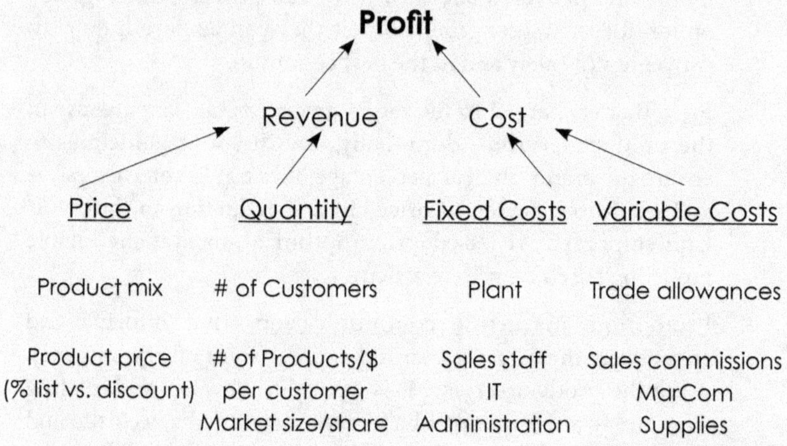

10. <u>Pivot</u> which outlines the ability of the organization to shift direction to promising new markets for the brand. This requires keeping up with changes in the business environment and customers not only in the specific areas of the SME's products and services but with other changes.

SME Story – Intro: Trajectory Brands Inc.

The art of being ahead of trends, operating interdependently and thinking and working systematically.

Trajectory Brands is a 13-year-old, Toronto based company operating in the marketing services industry. It provides both strategic and design consulting services for commercial, place, not-for-profit and government brand owners. Its current four partners, Peter Francey, Jeannette Hanna, Paul Hodgson and Stephen Weir, work with three other staff and a network of external partners to deliver Canada's most respected brand strategy advice and design solutions in Canada, the US and internationally.

Interview with Peter Francey and Jeannette Hanna, partners.

This highly successful $1.5 – $2 million revenue organization and its founding partners share a long history of learning and innovation in the brand marketing space. As this case reviews the group's evolution over more than four decades, several themes behind its success will be emphasized.

The Back-Story of Trajectory

The evolution of Trajectory goes back 45 years. By the late 1970s business partners Peter Francey and Clark Spencer had teamed up with writer/strategist Jeannette Hanna and designers Paul Hodgson and Gary Ludwig as principals of a successful graphic design business, Spencer Francey Group. In 1977 the founders set up their operation with a line of credit from a major Canadian bank local branch whose manager was convinced by their leading edge thinking and design Peter and Jeannette noted that much – if not most – thinking about brands and brand identity was both highly executional, lacking both good business strategy and anticipation of future changes and competition. Most was conducted by internal design departments, external advertising agencies or the occasional brand design specialist company In the 1980s they sold the company to a UK-based international marketing consultancy, Clarke Hooper, who had also acquired the Toronto office of The Michael Peters Group, a world-leading package design firm. With complementary corporate identity and packaging expertise, the two Toronto offices merged to form Spencer Francey Peters. However, a few years later when Clarke Hooper suffered economic fallout from the 1980s recession, the partners of Spencer Francey Peters were able to buy back the company By 2004 they had built a highly profitable $6 million business with some 40 employees and a global reputation based on work for commercial clients like Four Seasons Hotels and Resorts and Scotiabank; government organizations like Canada Post; cultural organizations like the Royal Ontario Museum (ROM) and place branding projects for Washington, D.C. and others.

Seeking to expand more internationally and integrate its activities with other areas of marketing communications, in 2004 they sold to the rapidly emerging integrated marketing communications agency Cundari, and CundariSFP with Peter Francey as its President was formed.

Over time the SFP partners found their ambitions and working culture were not working as well as part of the Cundari operation, so in 2009 they left to form Trajectory. Again, based on their strong reputation, thinking and design, early funds came from a line of credit from another major Canadian bank local branch.

Trajectory's new *modus operandi* evolved from insights Jeannette had gleaned as the lead author of a ground-breaking book in 2008 on brands titled *"Ikonica"*. The Trajectory name reflected how they would work with and for clients:

"Every client is on a unique trajectory based on where they've come from, where they are currently, and their ambitions for the future. Our role is to understand what it will take to fuel their next phase of development as a holistic brand that connects commerce, culture and community."

During their history they have built a global reputation in the strategy and execution of brand thinking in general, embraced the growing application of digital technology in their thinking and activity, and pioneered work in place and attraction branding internationally.

Learning from Trajectory

Amongst their many talents and successes, Trajectory demonstrate the power of attending to the following principles:

1. Attend to customer/client current and future needs in their business.

2. Stay current, study and anticipate changes in the commercial, ecological and socio-economic environment.

3. Build a positive and interdependent working culture internally and with outside suppliers and relationships so that holistic solutions can be developed. Systems integration is an important concept at Trajectory.

4. Build networks and contact in both business and volunteer work especially in leading edge and thought leadership groups.

5. Experiment with management and funding forms that fit both the ambitions and organization culture.

Let's briefly look at each of these. The first two are done together as part of the strategic assessment and design development work for their clients.

1. Attend to customer/client current and future needs in their business.

2. Stay current, study and anticipate changes in the commercial, ecological, and socio-economic environment.

Too many enterprises develop products/services based on their own understanding of their target customer's needs and do not do sufficient research and investigation to what is really going on with them. Even the good ones too often stop there and do not spend sufficient effort in reviewing developments elsewhere, for example, alternative industries and their solutions; developments globally and so on.

One big US win, Analog Devices, exemplified this.

Peter commented on the Analog win:

"...they told us they had looked at proposals from three big, big names in the States and it was like the same 'deck' coming off the shelf. They felt we had put together a much more intuitive plan that was really geared to their needs, more customized to them. Plus, they would get more attention from us than the others."

In terms of future thinking and trends, Jeannette describes part of the role of Peter and herself as being the 'scouts' of trends in their environment and the competition. This is aided by reaching out globally to potential suppliers and partners to set up reciprocal relations, plus their involvement in leading sector organizations. Peter, for example, was the prime mover in making Toronto the first international chapter of the Urban Land Institute, a prominent US think tank. He spearheaded a partnership with Canadian Business to create an annual ranking for Canada's Best Managed Brands. Jeannette served on the Board of the Boston-based Design Management Institute for nearly a decade, and is an expert panel member for two international professional hubs – the Placebrand Observer and CityNationPlace.

3. Build a positive and interdependent working culture internally and with outside suppliers and relationships so that holistic solutions can be developed. Systems integration is an important concept at Trajectory.

Their working culture has a long history of the core group having different roles and different skills which they all respect and work with. Peter rates the culture of their various organizations in their evolution as key to their ongoing success:

"It was very complementary and not competitive, and gave us strengths in a number of areas. Each of the partners has contributed to creating a robust culture and giving back to the community. Paul Hodgson, for example, taught for many years as an instructor at OCAD, inspiring next generation designers."

This is the very attitude they took to working with their external suppliers. As Peter and Jeannette commented, although they now have a total staff of seven:

"We use a lot of partners in areas where we need them like some digital areas, extra help on the design side especially interactive design, 3D designs and animation, social media, augmented reality and so on."

The other element that grew to mark SFP and then Trajectory's difference was brand thinking that had rigor and discipline as well as a more holistic and systematic approach. Led by Jeannette, this style appealed to all partners in their approach to brand thinking across corporate identity, packaging, internal communications, and external marketing communication - both off-line and on-line.

As Jeannette commented:

"The rise of the internet and digital design throughout the late 1980s and 1990s meant that you had to think about brands like a complex ecosystem. of relationships, experiences and stories."

Peter pointed out that this came even more into focus when they started work with Four Seasons Hotels and Resorts:

"Initially they hired us to do a lot of design work for them: collateral pieces and the like. But it dawned on us that they weren't selling hotel and resort rooms, but were selling the idea of luxury. Then that opened a whole way of talking about stories about their brand."

4. Build networks and contacts in both businesses and volunteer work especially in leading edge and thoughtful groups.

Trajectory had kept contact with previous clients they had worked with, and had a good reputation but as Jeannette commented:

"...much of our work, especially in place-branding, healthcare, education, and arts and culture is RFP driven. So, much of the early work was hustling for RFPs and working on those. The advantages we had was being small, nimble and working with a great roster of collaborators that we had worked with in the past. That enabled us to offer highly tailored services to fit customer needs."

For contacts in the U.S. and Canada, Trajectory subscribes to several search engines that list RFPs and look for those that fit their focus of brand activity and prior experience. In Canada it was a combination of contacts and RFP listings.

The early hard work and insight paid off quickly. Trajectory picked up brand work from Mount Allison University and then in 2010 the brand work for the upcoming Pan Am and Parapan Games scheduled for 2015 in Toronto. In the US, previous work for the Capitol Riverfront Neighborhood in Washington, DC paid off with several important contracts for Washington, DC. as well as the big contract for Analog Devices.

"In the US it was RFPs and relationships that built the business and constant attention to both. The 'third pillar' was being involved in sector-based associations, speaking at conferences and writing articles where we could build credibility with potential clients."

Then the issue is to stay in touch with those relationships. Jeannette points out Peter's strength in this aspect:

"Peter is fantastic at building relationships. One client said to him you've been in closer touch with me than my family. Close relationships help when clients move jobs or they refer you to others. People have said, although you haven't done work in this specific sector before, I trust you guys and your process to figure it out."

5. Experiment with management and funding forms that fit both the ambitions and the organizational culture.

They are able to try new ownership and management structures because of the trust between the partners. As Peter expresses it:

"Nobody is going to take us somewhere too dangerous for our business and our culture. We will always pull back just shy of the edge of the cliff, but let's at least look at the edge of the cliff to see how far we can go."

Peter does attest that thinking about planning the future is a big issue for SMEs and admits that they have experimented in the past, mostly successfully, but when it was evident that a direction didn't fit their culture, had the strength to change it.

Final thoughts from Trajectory

According to Peter and Jeannette:

"It does take a certain headstrong character to keep problem solving. It's not just luck, it's that constant looking for a way to tackle short- term problems or to seize emerging opportunities. You must constantly be noting what door has closed, and what door is opening somewhere else.

It's helpful not working solo and having partners you trust. We are a diverse group so whether you view the glass as half empty or half full, the debate is lively but positive because there is a belief in each other.

We are a learning organization and we continue on our learning journey. It's okay not to know all the answers. What's important is asking the right questions. Don't always accept the given wisdom of what's possible. Be curious and explore."

Interview January 3rd 2022.

1

SME MARKETING CHALLENGE #1: TARGET GROUP: CUSTOMER AND POTENTIAL CUSTOMER KNOWLEDGE

"Amazing things will happen when you listen to the consumer."

Jonathan Mildenhall, 1967 – date. American, CEO Twenty First Century Brand Consulting, ex- CMO Airbnb.

At the centre of business success lies both the concept/core idea for the product/service, and the identification of the target group who could be attracted to pay money to access that concept/idea.

Target groups for businesses range from very small in number but with a premium price, to very large with a lower price. The key is to understand who represents the best prospect and where to position the enterprise on this price/value continuum. This thinking should be done by considering local, national and international prospects. Some products/services can start with a local and national focus but many in this age of globally shared technology can be considered international right from the start as Shopify did: a company now operating with clients in 175 countries.

Ideally the development of the product/service and a view on who the target group for it is should be done together. Sometimes though one precedes the other, however both together should drive business decisions. One Russian SME I was training had developed new laser technology and was working on eleven different applications with eleven different target groups and not making any commercial progress. Through the training we identified two priorities and he has been hugely successful since.

So, what information do you need to know?

Keys to optimal selection of a target group strategy are the following six questions:

1. Research to provide identification of the most likely prospects and their numbers.

2. Research to provide understanding of these prospects in terms of attitudes and behaviors as they impact use and purchase decisions.

3. Research on what competitive products/services the prospects are currently using and their reasons are for satisfaction or dissatisfaction with these.

4. Research on how the prospects respond to the SME's product/service and its prospective price.

5. Research about how prospects would buy or source the product/service: the distribution strategy.

6. Ongoing research on the strengths and weaknesses of the brand proposition over time and relative to its competition.

Through this research it will be important to identify how adoption of the product/service will develop: who the innovators/early adopters will be, how their experience will impact the early majority of potential customers, and how quickly. In many of the SME Stories in this book you will find the research that has been carried out, from a micro site like Awoke N'Aware to larger organizations like Harry Rosen.

To help, the SME Marketing Challenge Tool #1: Target Group, should help define the kind of data and techniques to learn it.

SME Marketing Challenge Tool #1: Target Group

For B2C businesses:

- Demographic description: age; gender, family status (single, married, children); location (regions and urban/rural), work status, income if possible.

- Insight into home/work/personal lifestyle balance.

- Current product/service ownership/use, benefit(s) sought.

- Shopping habits: frequency of purchase and use. How purchased: retailers? online? Home delivery and/or store/site visits? Banners visited?

- Attitudes and values towards the products and services and how they fit in their lives.

- Pricing sensitivity for the specific product/service.

- Media/Social media habits.

- If a current client, level of loyalty and satisfaction.

- Competitive products/services as seen by the target group – these may be not only direct competitors but substitutes.

For B2B businesses, it will be similar kind of data but focused on:

- The business organization: small, medium, large. Ownership. Type of business (manufacturing, retail, service etc.). Location. Apparent financial situation.

- Peaks and valleys in demand in their business and why (weather? state of the national economy? Regulation etc.).

- Competition: current suppliers and any knowledge of level of integration with work processes and level of satisfaction.

- Supply chain and logistics issues: delivery and pricing preferences and sensitivities.

- Purchasing policies and approaches (bid systems, contracts etc.).

- If a current client, level of loyalty and satisfaction.

- Ambitions, changes and challenges facing the client.

Gathering the Data.

This may sound expensive and only for large organizations. It isn't. Also, while it is sometimes easier to do the research locally rather than internationally, this should not be an excuse to do none given the global world we inhabit and the opportunities that may lie offshore. The remainder of this tool tries to provide some thoughts on how to add this target group knowledge without huge expenditure.

1. <u>Direct Personal Contact</u>: SME principals should meet, talk to, and watch people they think might be interested in their product/service. They should watch how they work/shop using products/services that the SME product/service seeks to replace; understand how they talk about them, any rituals and of course what improvements or alternatives that would improve the performance. Research Rule one: spend time with those using the product/service the SME seeks to replace in the context of their use and purchase of the product/service.

2. <u>Meetings and Networking</u>: while this type of investigation may not be academically reliable or projectable to the full target group population, it can provide enormous value in both knowledge and contacts. Attendance, on-line or in-person, at Conferences, Trade Shows, relevant Trade Association meetings, Government run or sponsored events, and privately run events from organizations like the Business Development Bank of Canada (BDC) all have value. Additionally, keeping in touch with customers and potential customers via social media is a good way to listen to their views but also monitor competitors, and track trends. The key to gaining

value from these is, without giving away the intellectual property of the product/service, to ask questions, follow up and write-up/record data and observations.

3. <u>Secondary Research:</u> this is research that other groups have commissioned and published on-line or in hard copy. Nowadays this is so much easier to access than even a decade ago: there is just so much available on-line for low or no cost. The key is to find sources that are credible which means attention to who collected the data ('source credibility') and how and when it was collected ('data credibility'). On one project I was commissioned to discover the total size of a potential market in North America: I put in a quotation for $20,000 to do the research which was approved. When I started, I discovered a report had been produced from a credible source, with good data and published just 4 weeks earlier. The cost of the report was $1,500. I phoned the client and charged them $2,000 for the report and my assessment of it. Lost income for me yes, but a lesson for all on the wide availability of available data.

4. <u>Primary Research:</u> this is formal research the SME can commission. It can be qualitative to give insight and understanding or quantitative to deliver reliable and projectable data. Many research companies and private contractors are available to help with this: the largest Canadian owned market research company is Leger who run regular panel surveys that SMEs can buy into for low cost.

There are low-cost ways of doing research and gathering data and insights in various forms domestically and internationally.

- There are some 50 organizations that help organizations design, deliver, and analyze market research themselves. These include organizations such as Ask Nicely, Qualtrics, Snap Survey, Survey Monkey, Survey Sparrow, and many others.

- Many Federal, Provincial and Municipal Government organizations here in Canada and internationally have groups that for low or no cost, help with research investigations and reports to help SMEs investigate markets. Canada has the Trade Commission Service (TCS) with its 160 offices domestically and internationally. Additionally, there is Export Development Canada (EDC), an extremely well-regarded organization, and there are Provincial equivalents. Internationally many government trade offices provide free data and assistance. Examples include Japan External Trade Organization (JETRO), UK Department for International Trade Canada, and US Commercial Services in Canada (export. gov).

- Chambers of Commerce, not only the Canadian Chambers but many international Chambers operate to help overseas business: Toronto alone has Brazil-Canada, European Union and German Chambers.

- There are many independently run bilateral business societies that can provide data and information but also importantly networking opportunities with nationals from those countries. Personally, I have been directly involved with Canada-China Business Council (CCBC), Canada-India Business Council, Canada-Japan Society and others.

- Then there is the research help and input that can be provided by students at Universities and Colleges as part of their course work and internship activities. Contact with marketing faculty can often facilitate this, options include:

  - Individual student assignments during marketing courses.

  - Group student assignments during marketing courses.

  - Group assignments for courses such as Schulich School of Business Strategy Study.

  - Paid Individual or group assignments for programs like the York Consulting Group at Schulich School of Business.

The point is that there are many sources to gather the research and information needed to answer the six research questions posed at the beginning of this piece. These six provide part of the core to future business success.

SME Story 1.1. Awoke N'Aware Inc.

The art of how two partners successfully research, and plan a 'start-up' a microenterprise.

Awoke N' Aware Inc is a 3 – year old Toronto based company operating in the socially responsible fashion industry. It provides 'street-fashion' leisure clothing made from eco-friendly fabrics and recycled plastic and donates 15%+ of profits to support conservancies for elephants, rhinos and polar bears. In later developments they created an Ocean Edition created from recycled plastics that supports ocean clean up missions. The founding partners Kelly Saltzman and Cory Yefet work with international external suppliers of clothing but conduct all planning and execution themselves.

Interview with Kelly Saltzman and Cory Yefet.

Conceived and researched during 2018, then founded in 2019, Awoke N' Aware is a sustainable and ethical apparel brand on a mission to help our vulnerable planet. It starts with products made with eco-friendly fabrics such as organic cotton and later introduced recycled and upcycled materials. Additionally, it donates at 15% of its profits to international organizations that work to protect endangered species like elephants, rhinos and polar bears as well as ocean clean-up missions.

As Kelly indicates on their web site:

"It's not every day that your clothing purchase can help save some rhinos."

The birth of Awoke N' Aware.

The two young founders have different but complementary backgrounds. Kelly Saltzman worked for major marketing companies like General Mills and Shopify and is an MBA from the Schulich School of Business. Corey Yefet has spent 6 years working for various 'tech' start-ups like Top Hat, Uberflip and Home Stars. The two were on a vacation together and started talking about a 'start-up' enterprise together, especially to do with animals. The initial concept was an eco-friendly sweatshirt that funds could give back to animal preservation. The hypothesis was that, as Kelly put it:" *...that people were as obsessed with animals as I am"*. Cory had *"a very large interest in fashion and in entrepreneurship; I come from a family of entrepreneurs"*.

On return from vacation, they started:

"We jumped into research. What was the competitive landscape and then how do other people build businesses? This led us to the first concrete thing we did which was to build a business plan. We went out and found a few different resources, like Futurpreneur, our families, faculty at the business school, and podcasts that were available to answer questions like how to incorporate and other fundamentals."

They also talked to successful companies in the eco-fashion business: Ivory Ella and particularly Tentree were open and helpful.

They got a whiteboard and as Cory described it:

"This is where Kelly and I really went back and forth. We went through, where can we have the most impact? Let's put everything on the table and let's go through a process of elimination. On fashion items, we tried to identify industry trends: where is the market now, and then try to predict what might happen."

They decided on a limited clothing offering of primarily T-shirts but also sweatshirts/'hoodies. The animals they chose were Polar bears because of the Canadian connection, elephants and rhinoceros (rhinos) based on a combination of perceived popularity and the endangerment threat. Based on donating a share of their profits to animal organizations they made agreements with groups like the Ol Pejeta Conservancy which works to protect endangered species like rhinos.

Their target group originally was primarily young (18 – 30 years old) and women. It was also 50+ which emerged as a growth segment as grandparent – grandchild presents.

They had decided to self-fund through money saved as part of their regular jobs.

The launch of Awoke N' Aware

Following the business plan, they started the search for manufacturing. They pulled together a spreadsheet of 150 – 200 factories and started to narrow it down:

"We want it to be organic; to be ethical practice. We then set up guardrails on what we wanted to build."

They had decided their main offering would be T-shirts, but they also offered sweatshirts, hoodies and scrunchies (hair fasteners).

They eventually sourced from four suppliers: Metawear in India; Alternative Apparel and Royal Apparel in the US and one in Canada. Each order was around 1200 pieces at an average cost of US$6/T-shirt so they were spending US$ 7,200 per shipped order.

They decided that their first sales efforts would be direct sales at important Toronto shows relevant to their eco-friendly sector. The big first one was the "Green Living Show" at the Metro Toronto Convention Centre. It was a huge success. They were selling $5k/day and were exhausted but optimistic. So, they went on to other shows like "The Veg. Fest" at Fort York and "The Sustainable Block Party" in the Junction. Equally successful. The Summer 2019 launch went really well and although the Fall was a slower pace, sales continued well at some shows and on-line. On average, at around US$40/item they were getting gross sales of around $20k/month in peak months. They started to plan hiring a sales staff and traveling across North America to shows.

Pandemic Impacts

In March/April 2020 the pandemic hit. The shows that had been such a success for them in 2019 were canceled and they decided to speed up their move to online sales. This they did with interns from the Schulich School of Business who helped them with their on-line sales and marketing communications activity.

They had also contracted an advertising agency at this point to help boost their marketing communications activity and build brand awareness.

While their orders did slow down, they had purchased the clothes in bulk for better pricing, (stored at their home!) so they had sufficient stock. Sales volumes recovered. The pattern of demand surprised them: about 70% of sales were elephants, 25% rhinos and only 5% polar bears. They then introduced their Ocean Edition line from recycled plastics where 15% of profits went to ocean clean up missions.

Things were going well and as Kelly says:

"We started thinking about the future for us. We knew if we put in the time there was a real, viable business for us. We knew there was a market

for us and we'd learned so much. So, we were thinking about how this fitted our plans to be involved in several enterprises."

Based on that thinking, and changes in their personal and work lives, by the end of 2021 they had sold to one of their interns and now seek to apply their learning in new areas.

What worked?

1.   The partners teamwork.

To quote Cory:

"One thing that worked really well is that we accepted what each of us was good at. I knew Kelly was good at, and she accepted what I was good at, and we didn't really overlap."

2.   A customer focus.

The other area of learning was from an error of overinvesting in an early supplier and their product rather than really listening to the customer, as Kelly said:

".... having smaller, more limited runs that were more flexible in meeting customer preferences."

This is what then worked for them as the initial Consumer shows took place.

What didn't work so well?

1.   Too complex an offering for a small enterprise.

In hindsight, Cory felt they should have focused more in the variety of their offerings:

"The competitive landscape told us that we should have focused on one thing and we chose to do several. It cost us too much to promote each of the lines and their stories. With elephants alone, although most competitive, the demand rate was so high we could comfortably have seen a couple of million sales a year."

2.   Getting distracted from the business plan focus.

Kelly talks about 'the shiny objects' trap. Areas unattractive or even dangerous to the enterprise that look so inviting but on closer examination may not be:

"If you just want short term success, it is so easy to get distracted by shiny objects that detract you from your goal."

3. Be clear about your marketing communications goals and supplier.

Cory had a view on using advertising agencies:

"I think we overinvested in advertising and underinvested in performance marketing. Performance marketing had the potential for the greatest ROI but we were so passionate about what people will look at when they see our brand rather than focus on what communication will make some sales."

Interview January 12th 2022

2

SME MARKETING CHALLENGE #2: BUILDING YOUR SUSTAINABLE BRAND

*"A brand for a company is like a reputation for a person.
You can earn a reputation by trying to do hard things well."*

"Your brand is what people say about you when you are not in the room."

Jeff Bezos, 1964 – date. American entrepreneur, founder of Amazon and Blue Origin.

Successful sales and marketing is not just about short-term sales success but, importantly, sustaining and growing profitable sales over the longer term. This means building a major business asset: a strong brand.

A brand is not just a name, it is an important asset for the organization that helps:

- Build knowledge and exposure of the product/service and its value to the customer and potential customer.

- Helps build an emotional as well as utilitarian connection.

- When done well, reduces price sensitivity.

- Helps build customer loyalty and repeat purchase.

- Thereby helps profitability, and becomes a valued asset for the business.

Brands are a significant financial asset of public corporations: their value averaged 20% of total market capitalization in a survey of 300 companies done from 2010-2015 (source Jonathan Knowles) but even higher in consumer services (44%); consumer durables and automotive (34%); retailing and software (27%); food, beverage and tobacco (25%); telecommunications (24%); household & personal products (21%).

"Big brands are well known and respected. In Canada based on the Leger 2022 Reputation Study, Canadians buy and highly respect local brands like Shoppers Drug Mart (a net respect score of 73% and #1 rank); Canadian Tire (a net score of 71% and #4 rank); as well as Dollarama, McCain, Maple Leaf, Chapters Indigo, Sobeys and Purolator who are all over 58% and in the top 30 ranked in Canada.

So, what is a brand? What goes into building a strong brand?

My definition is "to its target group it is a promise of benefits consistently delivered with a high level of value and satisfaction versus direct and indirect competitors." Another commentator, David Kincaid at Level 5 brand consultants define it as "The value of a promise consistently kept."

Delivering that promise requires the coordination of multiple elements and their constant improvement over time. These include the name and the organization it comes from and its logo/symbol. In thinking ahead, SMEs should make sure that name and logo are acceptable in a multi-cultural world not only in recognition of Canada's diversity but also in anticipation of potential international markets. This means finding a brand name and logo (and a URL) that are not insulting or negative in another language, that express the brand proposition and that are registrable (and therefore protectable) in countries of interest.

In addition to the brand name and logo the brand promise also includes the product/service itself (design and performance); any packaging; for retailers the design and utility of the physical space and the on-line website. It includes the price (both regular and "deal" price) to deliver the benefit/cost value proposition; the distribution that enables easy purchase access and the credible reputation of the providers of that access; and customer service levels delivered before, during and after purchase. It also includes the content and style of its sales and marketing communications (advertising: both digital and non-digital, PR, and promotional activity). Critical to the delivery of all of this is employee and distributor knowledge and behavior: not just knowledge of the brand's function but its full promise.

Even with effective management of the brand promise, external events such as competitive activity in providing alternatives or substitutes, and changes in technology and legislation require constant anticipation of changes to the brand and innovation in all areas. Nowadays this "market scanning" activity must be local and international. Despite customs duties and other regulatory advantages given to local SMEs, competition is fully global so international competitors' activities should also be tracked. The other side of this coin is that this examination may point to international opportunities for the SME. ("SME Marketing Challenge #1: Customer and Potential Customer Knowledge", the previous chapter provided some tips on how to go about this research).

Strong brands are built with attention to not only utilitarian benefits but also to what appeals to the senses and the emotion. In what is known as the "Notice. Believe. Feel." paradigm, great brands' value proposition includes:

Notice: what the customer notices about the brand from the 5 senses: sight, sound, smell, taste, touch. This includes the actual product/service design and any packaging.

Believe: what the customer believes about the brand from any reasoned, factual or rational arguments. This could be performance data, product/service design data, customer satisfaction data, sustainability data and so on.

Feel: what the customer feels about the brand from the emotion, sometimes termed "affect". The range of emotions is large so the specific emotion must be based on the appeal to the target group. 15 types of affect have been identified as used in marketing: interest/expectancy, surprise, disgust/scorn, skepticism, anger, fear/anxiety, shame, guilt, pity, pride, sadness, social affection, drives (e.g., pain, fatigue), deactivation ("quiet pleasure"), SEVA – Surgency, Elation, Vigor/Activation (active joy). Research has shown emotional appeals vary in their importance by product/service category. In consumer goods for example research indicates the importance of emotion in driving purchase ranges from a low of 30% in categories like non-prescription pharmaceuticals, to a high of over 60% in categories like beer and alcoholic beverages and fast-food restaurants. As the SME Story of Nature's Path shows later in this chapter, it is a key in food marketing in general.

It is helpful for SMEs to develop their brand proposition concurrently with the development of the product/service. The Brand Value Proposition format can be used to write up the thinking and research.

SME Marketing Challenge Tool #2:
The Brand Value Proposition

Part 1: What the Brand is.

For: define the target market: location, demographics, attitudinal data, what products/services are they currently using. And why

Who Want: benefits: define what problems are solved/advantages in the target group's lives by the SME's brand and the product/service

Our product/service is: describe the product/service and what solution it provides to meet the target group's needs/desires

Our other features: what other aspects of your brand are important: user ratings, influencers, distribution extensiveness, price/vale etc

Key features: define the key benefit provided

As measured by: how will buyers know you have these benefits: Performance data? Design? Statement? Endorsement?

Part 2. Why we will win.

Unlike: define and describe the main competitors locally and in major international markets

Our Brand provides: describe what you know or have researched as the key points of difference: Notice, Believe, Feel.

- <u>Notice</u>: from the <u>senses</u> (sight, sound, smell, taste, touch) what do you want your target group to <u>experience</u> about the brand's product/service and its presentation compared to its competition: e.g., the product look, feel and smell, the packaging, display material etc.

- <u>Believe</u>: from <u>thought and analysis</u> what do you want your target group to <u>believe</u> about the brand compared to its competition: e.g., its formula; technology; public or influencer group acceptance and use etc.

- <u>Feel: emotionally</u> what do you want your target group to <u>feel</u> about the brand compared to its competition: e.g., more contemporary; more trusted; exciting; reliable etc.

As supported by: what makes our difference possible: Unique technology? Better ingredients? Better manufacture or assembly? Lower cost ingredients/labour? Greater trust from previous activities or endorsements? Etc

As promoted by: what are you doing to sell and advertise and promote your brand either digitally or in other media? Does the message convey your distinctiveness and its benefits? Does the media you use reach the right targets? Are you spending enough relative to competition? Are you measuring the effectiveness of your promotion activities?

And available at: are you available in places on-line and off-line convenient for your customers?

And protected by: why can't competition easily overcome your advantage? What is it that you have or are doing that sustains your advantage?

Find ways to constantly improve: what are you doing to constantly improve your internal and external business processes so that you can improve your value proposition?

Strongly connected to how successful a brand is and can become is its positioning which is the result of the 10 factors in the marketing mix described earlier.

The brand experience is the totality of what the target segment perceives and receives before, during and after the purchase.

Positioning is the way you want your customers to store this experience in the mind of the target segment. It defines the framework for the market and puts your experience to work to identify:

- Who is the target market?

- What your target market wants/needs?

- Who is the competition?

- What are the most desired attributes/benefits in the category?

- What is your competitive position on these desired attributes/benefits?

This is often shown in a data sourced chart – called a perceptual map – that plots your brand versus competition on the key desired rational and emotional attributes:

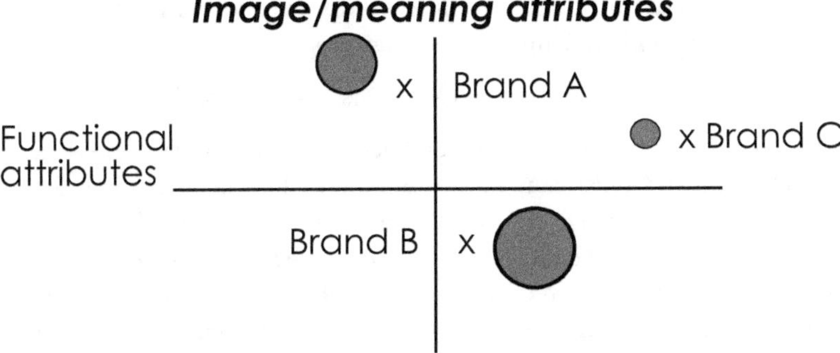

The data is used to determine the size of the different segments and what areas you and the competition inhabit relative to the size of those segments, this enables you to adjust the brand marketing mix appropriately to achieve an optimal positioning.

The challenge is to build both your short-term sales and margin and also the power and positioning of your brand so that you have a successfully growing Canadian company like Nature's Path Foods.

SME Story # 2. Nature's Path Foods

A successful, family-owned enterprise that has grown from small, to medium to large in its under 40 years of existence. Its business is growing, manufacturing and selling often unique, vegetarian, certified organic and non-GMO cereals and other foods. Nature's Path is a triple bottom line social enterprise recognized through numerous awards for incorporating sustainability into its business practices.

Founded in 1985 in Richmond, B.C. by husband-and-wife team Arran and Ratana Stephens, Nature's Path is approximately a $500 million/year revenue organization that employs around 800 people

and sells more than 150 products, primarily in the US and Canada but also internationally. They own a 5,000-acre organic farm in Saskatchewan, and four manufacturing facilities in Canada and the US. They operate with zero-waste certification, have committed to carbon neutrality and are active supporters of many social sustainability and environmental programs.

Interview with Arran and Ratana Stephens, founders and co-owners.

Early days for Arran and Ratana go back to organic berry and sweet corn farming in Goldstream, B.C for Arran; teaching at college in India for Ratana, and a strongly held belief that they should jointly follow the advice passed on by Arran's father, to *"Always leave the soil better than when you found it"*. Based on this combination of expertise in organic farming, and belief, Arran opened Canada's first vegetarian restaurant in 1967. In 1969 Ratana joined him in the business. Then in 1971 they opened a natural foods store, then distributor, and then producer of organic foods called 'Lifestream Natural Foods'.

As Arran said:

"I felt intuitively that the time would come when organic foods would become the norm. Inevitably it would attract big competitors and I wanted to ensure that we would be there when that happened."

One of the first products Lifestream made was 'Essene Bread R' a bread made exclusively from fully sprouted, organic whole wheat kernels. They were real pioneers: Arran estimates that the total organic food market was only around \$1 – 2 million sales in Canada and the US in the late 1960s. However, their early success and belief encouraged them to go further and in 1985 Nature's Path was founded out of the back of their 120 - seat vegetarian restaurant in Vancouver.

Early funding for Nature's Path came from surplus from both their profitable restaurant and mortgaging their home which enabled them to explore and then launch organic cereals. On April 6th 1989 they took a major step forward and, despite no former experience, opened North America's first certified organic cereal plant - in Delta, B.C. That it was not easy is an understatement. As Arran says:

"There was a LOT of difficulty. Because we didn't know how to make ready-to-eat cereals in a factory setting, we learned from mistake after mistake. We learned to make cereal differently from all our competitors

and that made all the difference. Our cereal doesn't get soggy in milk like the major non-organic brands, it has a different taste, texture and nutritional profile. It's always been whole grain, organic, and with much lower sugar content – unlike others."

They plowed all earnings back into the company, Arran did not take a salary for the first year. Ratana ran the restaurant, which as Arran says, *"kept us afloat".*

By 1993 Nature's Path rose to become the North American brand leaders in organic breakfast cereal - they expanded their product range:

"We got into granola, then toaster pastries and so on."

The next three decades saw continued expansion and growth. From 1992 Ratana's role changed from running the restaurant to becoming fully engaged with Arran in running Nature's Path, in fact she is currently the CEO. The work was a constant learning and problem-solving journey.

"We grew by winning customers one at a time with our high-quality products and by their word of mouth."

This journey included acquisition in 2017 of Que Pasa, a family-owned company whose principals wanted to retire.

"A certified organic company that made tortilla chips, not with flour but whole organic corn which is soaked and ground using real volcanic millstones from Mexico. This makes them much more nutritious and flavourful than those made from corn flour"

In product terms Nature's Path remains primarily an organic cereal provider: about 80% of their business is organic cereals and granola. However, by a combination of growth, innovation and acquisition their product range has increased. Under the Nature's Path brand, they market cereal, granola and bars, oatmeal, chips and salsa, toaster pastries and waffles. Under the Que Pasa brand they offer tortilla chips and salsa. Under Qi'a they offer plant-based and healthy fats cereals and oatmeal. Under EnviroKidz they offer healthy cereals and waffles for kids. Under Love Crunch, a brand developed by their son Arjan and his wife Rimjhim, they offer premium granola bars and cereal

In November 2021 Nature's Path acquired an 80% interest in one of their ingredient suppliers, Anita's Organic Mill in Chilliwack, BC.

Anita's is developing a strong retail presence with its organic pancake mixes.

Currently about 75% of their business is in the US, 21% and freshly milled flours in Canada, and 4% internationally. Almost all products are sold under their own brand names, though they do supply limited private label for Trader Joe's in the US and two products grandfathered in at Loblaws in Canada. The focus of Nature's Path and Que Pasa is brand building not private label. As Arran says:

"In the absence of a brand, price becomes the brand."

Their growth has been aided by an increased society-wide focus on healthier foods and environmental issues. It is estimated that the organic foods market is now worth around US$110 billion/year. Nature's Path saw this need and opportunity early and has innovated its way forward. While their marketing efforts at the beginning were limited, the effort has grown: they now have a significant marketing team. At the core of their marketing proposition has been the quality, organic purity and uniqueness of their products. As Ratana says:

"The quality of our products is everything. Quality is priority #1. Quality is priority #2. Quality is priority #3."

They have always been leaders and pioneers in their product offerings. In addition to trade shows and sales force calling on retailers they now more actively promote in social media. Cost of goods is a big issue in organics. While a small premium price is possible for organic foods, it does not fully cover the higher raw costs. First, cost of raw materials is 20% – 100% higher than non-organic equivalents. Second, certified organic plant operations are more complex and more expensive to run.

In production they expanded from one plant in Delta, BC, to two others in the US: Sussex, Wisconsin (the biggest) and Blaine, Washington State. They continue to search for additional facilities in Eastern Canada to meet increasing demand. Key personnel are the heads of their manufacturing facilities as they apply strict health, safety, sustainability and carbon neutral goals. They have developed many staff internally, one of their senior plant managers worked his way up from the shop floor. As Arran puts it:

"We grow our replacements".

Their growth has meant additional management hiring. Of Arran and Ratana's four children, two are actively engaged in the business and are set to succeed their parents. Arjan Stephens is the General Manager of Nature's Path Foods and President of Que Pasa Foods. He was instrumental in the launch of many of the new brands like Love Crunch, Qi'a and Nature's Path Sunrise Cereals, and in the acquisition of Que Pasa Foods. Jyoti Stephens, the youngest daughter, is Vice President of Mission and Strategy. She leads continuation and further commitment to sustainable agriculture, ethical sourcing, energy efficiency, waste reduction, community engagement and eco-friendly packaging. In addition, they have grown internal management talent: Arran says that in organics:

"We are both truth seekers and talent seekers. Everyone must always train their replacement."

Growth continues from established brands but also new acquisitions. As mentioned earlier, Nature's Path acquired a majority stake in Anita's Organic Mill, a highly respected miller and manufacturer of organic whole grain flour, pancake and other baking mixes.

"They supplied Nature's Path with bulk flour for several years. They needed money and expertise. They needed help in marketing and other areas, so we thought it was a great fit."

Nature's Path gained the expertise of the former owners and an additional plant. Anita's organic flour brands will continue to be marketed under the Anita's Organic brand name to the retail and industrial trade.

Future

Under the mantra that they must still make a difference, the organization continues to view growth as both a contribution to the ecosphere and a business need. Their past has been a constant history of overcoming problems and issues as they pioneered their way forward. Both Arran and Ratana recognize that this will continue. While there is likely continued growth in the demand for healthier foods and eco-friendly practices, challenges come in many forms. As Arran says:

"Who knows what the future holds, we are open to all possibilities, but it has to be synergistic and where the sum total is much greater than the parts."

Ratana is firm in her view:

"When we talk about our possibilities, it's not to be acquired but acquiring."

Challenges come in many forms. First big established cereal competitors moving more aggressively into the organics market. This requires constant upgrading of product, manufacturing efficiency and marketing. Second, labour shortages in all areas and with it the need for improvements in production and supply chain operations technology. Third, constant pricing pressures caused by increasing cost of raw materials and packaging, cost of transportation and costs of people.

Arran and Ratan point out:

"The business is never really a destination, it's always a journey. It never stays static. Life is not static."

Their pride comes from the fact that

"We played a pivotal role in the development of the organic movement: providing channels for farmers; providing good quality, healthy, tasty products to consumers."

Lessons from Nature's Path

First and so apparent with this company that pioneered organic formulas, manufacture and sales and distribution, was a fierce determination to keep going to deliver the vision, *"to make things better and to leave the earth better than we found it"*.

"One of the things that characterized the difference between our failures and our success is our stubbornness, our tenacity, our resiliency. Many others might have thrown in the towel faced with similar challenges. A success is a failure that never gave up."

Second, they invested in plant technology and other processes to continue to be competitive and deliver high quality products.

Third, they invested time and money in people to build expertise and a positive culture: as Ratana puts it:

"One with heart."

Fourth is the passion for the overall vision and mission to do things well for people and the planet. Every entrepreneur should be motivated by more than money, to set and achieve a motivating vision and mission. As Ratana says:

"Business is not only about money. It is about making a difference. It is about environmental and social responsibility."

Interview: January 31st 2022.

3

SME MARKETING CHALLENGE #3: DEVELOP AND STAFF A STRATEGIC AND OPERATIONAL MARKETING PLAN

"Tactics without strategy is the noise before defeat."

Sun Tsu; 544 BCE – 496 BCE; Chinese, author "The Art of War".

"Marketing Strategy is where we play how we will win in the market. Tactics are how we then deliver on the strategy and execute for success."

Mark Ritson PhD; British; Marketing scholar.

Developing the marketing plan should be done concurrently with the overall business plan and falls out of the overall Vision and Mission. The process can be seen in what is called the Strategic Hierarchy.

While management of this strategic and operational process is not simple, it need not be overly complicated. However, it does require commitment and skill. Many SMEs do not hire and/or listen to the required strong talent to make it work well and this is why despite the promise of great products/services, many Canadian SMEs do not achieve the success they should attain. A consistent feature of the SME Stories in this book has been the thinking, research and planning that has gone into their process. The marketing part of this process covers all aspects of marketing and seeks to ensure that the elements are not developed in isolation but in an integrated manner that builds a powerful brand proposition. The elements are the Marketing Mix 10 discussed earlier in the introduction.

The process of development of the Strategic Hierarchy should include data from the kind of research described in Chapter 2, and reflection, discussion and debate. Ideally this should be done amongst the partners and/or the senior management team. In this way alternative scenarios can be developed and examined before automatically jumping to linear conclusions that may not fit marketplace developments. Attention to the flow of the hierarchy, both vertically and horizontally, will help discipline the thinking. Readers will note the thoroughness of the process conducted by the SMEs in this book, from the Small size Awoke N'Aware and Diabetes Care Community, through the Medium size Hatley and Mother Raw to the now large Sleep Country.

SME Marketing Challenge Tool # 3:
The Strategy Hierarchy

Vision/Mission

- what you want to accomplish that provides a benefit to a set of customers in a way that delivers value to all stakeholders (shareholders, staff, suppliers, community)

Goals and Values

- what measurable achievements you want to attain to satisfy customers and stakeholders. What values you wish to bring to society and your organization.

Strategy

- how you will attain those goals: scope, scale, speed, cost/finance, marketing, brand, risk assessment

Resources, Culture and Structure

- the key enablers of the strategy

Tactics

- how you will specifically deliver components of the strategy: new products & services, acquire, merge, alliance, reorganize etc.

Implementation

- what you will do, when, by whom, with what resources and how you will measure achievement and then respond.

SME Story #3.1. Diabetes Care Community. (www.diabetescarecommunity.ca)

A small pioneering organization that runs a website and online resource for people with diabetes and prediabetes to source current medical, nutritional and other advice and knowledge.

Founded in Toronto in 2011 by Ian Gardner and Shelley Diamond, the Diabetes Care Community (DCC) is an on-line resource that offers expert advice and information on topics such as types of diabetes; diabetes in children; diabetes and seniors; managing type 2 diabetes; meal preparation; recipes; exercises; diabetes news and so on. With 80,000 unique visitors/month to its web site, spending an average of 3 minutes/page and almost 24,000 subscribers to their newsletter, they attract pharmaceutical and other advertisers seeking to build contact and relationships with these individuals and their families. Advertising revenue is presently just under $500k.

Interview with Ian Gardner, CEO and Co-Founder.

The Concept and Early Days

In 2008, Ian Gardner and Shelly Diamond met during some training and development work they were both doing for Shoppers Drug Mart to help them create a training program for pharmacists studying for Certified Diabetes Educator certification. Ian was a marketing communications specialist having spent over two decades working in advertising agencies such as McCann Erickson and Saatchi & Saatchi, and then his own consulting group Gardner & Associates specializing in healthcare, life sciences and pharmacy. Shelley Diamond, after graduation with a B.Sc.Phm, had worked as a Clinical and Drug Use Evaluation Pharmacist for the Hospital for Sick Children. After a decade there, she then set up her own healthcare consulting group, Pedipharm Consultants, where she consulted to large retail pharmacy chains like Shoppers Drug Mart and Loblaw pharmacy for over 15 years.

Working together on the pharmacist education program for Shoppers Drug Mart, they got talking about the future of healthcare. They became aware of the work of Tom Ferguson, an American MD and his work to have people use online services to help their own health: the concept of "e patients" had begun to emerge. They were inspired by his 2006 White Paper "e-patients. *How They Can Help Us Heal Healthcare.*"

They were struck by the issues surrounding the growth of both type 1 and type 2 diabetes incidence in Canada and around the world. An estimated 29% of the Canadian population live with prediabetes and diagnosed and undiagnosed diabetes: about 11 million people. The impact on the healthcare system was, and is, huge as there are major complications including heart attacks, kidney failure, as well as vision issues and feet and leg problems. Furthermore, they became aware that the health of the majority of people could be managed by proper diet and appropriate lifestyle in addition to medications such as metformin and insulin.

Ian comments:

"I believed the way to advocate for patients as an equal partner in their health journey was by providing trustworthy education and tools so that they could improve their knowledge and skills. Skills required to improve diabetes self-management capabilities and knowledge required to become an active partner in their health journey."

Additionally, he noted:

"No private company in Canada was focused on helping diabetes patients take better care of themselves, yet some examples existed in the US. Like dLife and diaTribe and TuDiabetes."

Based on this thinking and their experience Ian and Shelley did research and prepared a concept for an online health site for diabetes, and developed a prototype. Through their research they uncovered that while there was a strong need for a patient-centric approach to healthcare in Canada, there was also distrust of online information. Based on this they committed to bringing in experts on the topic and ones with appropriate qualifications. Through her extensive network of healthcare and diabetes experts, Shelley and her team built, and continue to build, a substantial inventory of reliable, trustworthy information on every aspect of diabetes self-management.

"We put together a team of healthcare professionals and medical writers, many of whom are still with us today."

The business model was for revenue to come from website and online newsletter advertising. They took the prototype to some pharmaceutical companies and strong interest was expressed. Start-up funds came from their consulting businesses, friends and family.

Based on this work and early interest, in September 2011 the Diabetes Care Community was launched. Ian and Shelley are the major shareholders and there are three other minority shareholders.

Growth and Learning.

With both the website and encouraging people to subscribe to their monthly mailing of *"Living Well with Diabetes,"* the Diabetes Care Community support system to help people manage their health better, was launched.

Through 2013/14 business was slow but steady. However, their marketing communications were not delivering strong results. They reached out to Igor Nesmyanovich at Technoscience (now branded Eradium), a data scientist. He helped Ian and Shelley gain a better understanding of the visitor's content requirements which significantly increased web traffic and over time improved visitor engagement. The intelligence gained from his firm's marketing insights helped make the articles, tools and information more targeted to the needs of the diabetes community.

"Probably one of the most important junctures in our business history. That's when the marketing communications really began to have an influence"

Shelley and their contracted team of expert contributors now meet regularly armed with better and timely information to create new content and new channels of communication. Over the years Ian and Shelley have used two contract medical writers, nine contract health professionals, and two contract marketing people. Time spent per page increased and all this aided a better story for advertisers.

"Our marketing team are in the marketplace on a day-to-day basis, finding out what people are looking for, what's important to them, their words and phrases. Every month we sit down with our analytics team and learn what's important, and translate that into new content, new articles, new channels. The marketing strategy is very focused on attracting people

to specific areas, to specific content and specific channels that will relate to what patients are looking for. When they come, there's a high degree of interest, a high degree of engagement, and they go, 'yes that's exactly what I was looking for!"

Gradually advertisers came on board and many have remained over the years. Diabetes Care Community's customers have been sourced from previous contacts and now, increasingly, healthcare conferences, LinkedIn and cold calls. Some of their current advertisers include Ascensia Diabetes Care Holdings, a subsidiary of the PHC Group; Dexcom a US based company providing continuous glucose monitoring devises; Novo Nordisk; Sanofi; Ypsomed Canada; Egg Farmers of Canada and others. Over time Ian has observed a change in advertiser's messages. It has moved from awareness and product conversion to a more consultative, educational, content - based approach.

As Ian comments, the perspective of advertisers is much more:

"We want to be your partners in diabetes care.

And that is the very vision of the Diabetes Care Community. We do it through education, through content, reaching out to them on a regular basis and asking what's of interest, what they want to hear, and how we can help."

Surveys done by Ipsos for the Society of Participatory Medicine have validated this approach.

In Canada the other major diabetes–based organization is Diabetes Canada. It is a registered national charity that develops the Canadian diabetes clinical practice guidelines and remains an excellent source of research and data, as well as doing patient advocacy with governments. There are no other organizations serving the 11 million Canadian community of those living with diabetes or prediabetes.

Recently DCC has been asked to submit a brief to a Federal Government Standing Committee "Dialogue on Diabetes", part of Bill C237 on the need for better funding for the study and development of a health strategy for diabetes. Internationally, including the US, there are many organizations like DCC, so the team constantly monitors and learns from their activities.

Future Developments/Challenges:

Become the preferred destination for people with diabetes and prediabetes and the number one newsletter. To do so by continuing to invest in gathering consumer views and information so that DCC stays in contact with the needs of the diabetic community

"While we are a profitable company, we are still at a point where we are reinvesting into our portal, into our content. Money into patient engagement. Money into new tools and applications to support a healthier diabetes community."

Improving the patient counselling system via "BetterDiabetesCare", a new, proprietary, web-based application from DCC, designed in consultation with Certified Diabetes Educators.

This is a priority for DCC. "BetterDiabetesCare" is a recently developed web-based application for healthcare professionals engaged in counselling people with diabetes and prediabetes.

Currently, education programs in Canada try to educate the patient on all aspects of diabetes management at once. This overwhelms and confuses the patient, especially those newly diagnosed. This current system does not empower the patient to develop self-management skills. At the same time, healthcare professionals engaged in diabetes education are time-starved and have limited resources to address the complex issues involved in diabetes self-management.

"The current education system – particularly for the newly diagnosed - overwhelms the patient with all the new behaviours: change your eating patterns, change your physical activity patterns, change your monitoring, change your medication etc. etc. They dispense all of this information, usually in one seminar, and say 'away you go, go behave differently'!!"

Research indicates that when people are confronted with complex issues and several required actions, they often do not change behaviours at all. A better way is to focus on one patient challenge at a time, and only when the challenge is overcome, move on to the next most important issue.

"BetterDiabetesCare" is a collaborative system whereby a healthcare professional and patient work on one challenge at a time to create a patient action plan to address this singular issue. The discussion is usually around 15 minutes duration. This is a data-driven discussion, pre-populated with common issues and matched to self-management recommendations and relevant sources from the educational content at DCC's knowledge portal.

"A bottom up rather than a top-down approach."

It would be positioned as a coach/mentor helping the patient with their particular journey to achieve better habits.

In the first quarter of 2021, the prototype was tested with patients and healthcare professionals. Four counselling sessions were conducted following quantitative and qualitative study. There was enthusiastic and energetic acceptance by both groups.

The business concept was to take the service to pharmacies, but the resurgence of COVID meant that pharmacies have been focused elsewhere. Medium–term though, with the growth in the importance and activities of pharmacies, Ian sees a need to build deeper relations and seek joint venture opportunities with DCC's knowledge and capabilities in training and patient centricity.

Lessons for SMEs:

- Stay close to your vision and mission.

- Keep upgrading your product and services.

- Stay ahead, or at minimum current, with changes in marketing and marketing communications effectiveness.

- Look for synergies and areas for cooperation in related areas.

Interview: February 8th 2022.

SME Story 3.2. Leger

A small, then medium, now the largest Canadian-owned market research and analytics company,

Founded in Montreal in 1986 by Jean-Marc Leger, they have grown to become one of Canada's premier market research organizations. With over 600 employees in seven offices across Canada, one in Philadelphia in the US, and revenues of around $52 million, Leger offers services in customized market research, panels, polling and analytics. They serve multiple sectors with particular strength in public affairs, healthcare and retail/consumer goods, but also substantial engagement in energy, financial services, telecommunications, tourism/leisure and transportation.

Interview with Jean-Marc Leger, Founder and President/CEO.

History

Founded in 1986 as Leger & Leger by Jean-Marc Leger, his father Marcel who was an ex-Quebec Government environment minister, and three employees, the organization was primarily a polling firm. Constantly reinvesting their project surpluses, they grew consistently over the next few years adding important staff: Anne-Marie Marois the current COO joined them in November 1990. They added additional market research capability until they gained a major $2.5 million contract for Health Quebec. This assignment for the Quebec Government during 1992 and 1993 involved personal interviews with some 60,000 Quebec citizens, and achieved a 75% response rate. This helped raise the profile of the organization, and by 1996 they had a profitable enterprise.

In 1996 following the sad death of Marcel, and the growth of their broader market research capability, they rebranded as Leger Marketing and began their national expansion. At the time, research organizations tended to be very regional, based on knowledge of local clients and their needs. As such their growth strategy was acquisition of regional research organizations with strong polling, research and analysis capabilities and local client contacts. As Jean-Marc says:

"There is a huge difference between Canada and the US. Canada is mainly a regional market. If you were not in Toronto or Vancouver you would not get Toronto or Vancouver business."

In 2000 they attracted an investor, the "Fonds de solidarite FTQ ", a development capital fund set up by the Quebec Government with the largest labour union to expand employment and Quebec enterprise. This helped Leger take a higher level of risk in their planning and in 2000 they acquired Criterion Research of Toronto. With the acquisition came the second in command, Dave Scholz, who is a Partner and Executive Vice President with Leger today. They continued westward with the acquisition of Criterion Research in Edmonton in 2005 and Claros Research in Calgary in 2006. In 2007 they entered the US market by acquiring ARC Research in Philadelphia.

Recognizing the changes in technology and forms of analysis, in 2005 the Leger Marketing Web division conducted its first online survey for a panel, one of the first in Canada, and now the largest. Their strategic planning set them to move from just research and polling to greater analysis, analytics, strategy and consulting and that led to new acquisition and developmental targets to further their expertise. In 2012 they took a majority shareholding in Agility Metrics of Montreal, a company built around a cloud computing application for measuring customer experience. Also, in that year they acquired Researchology, a Toronto-based market research firm specializing in pharmaceutical research. In 2013 they added to that expertise with the acquisition of Ifop, also specializing in the pharmaceutical and consumer goods sectors.

In 2013 they evolved their brand to Leger to reflect their broader capabilities and set up specialist divisions under the overall Leger brand. Internal growth and acquisitions of expertise and operations continued. In 2019 they completed the acquisition of the National Research Group with its Vancouver headquarters and offices in Calgary and Winnipeg. In 2020 Smartpoint Research in Toronto joined; in 2021 Ressac, a Montreal based digital performance agency and then Insights West, a Vancouver based research and analytics firm.

Jean-Marc charts the evolution of the industry in the following manner, which led Leger to make the moves it did:

"1970s: "What? the era of quantitative research.
1980s: "Why?" the era of qualitative alongside quantitative research.
1990s: "How?" the era of process: regression analysis research.

2000s: "Who?" segmentation studies and individual targeting research. 2010/2020s: "What if?" development of analytics research."

Leger's Expansion Strategy and Lessons for SMEs.

The strategy employed by the various Leger organizations consistently followed a number of principles to deliver a quality product and people first, then fun and profit.

"First we must be the best, then we will be the first."

So, as described earlier, the first priority was to build a national presence by acquisition of regional and specialist research organizations who brought with them high research expertise and local client contacts.

Second, to have research and analysis professionals as the key managers in charge of the client contracts.

"To be sure the client is well served, have researchers managing the business."

Third, to constantly innovate in the research and analytics field. Examples include the early online surveys and the development of the large Leger Opinion Panel (LEO); combining neuroscience learning with market research; early focus on digital performance metrics and others.

Fourth, a focus on staff and their motivation, training and development at all levels. At senior management the partners, ten of whom are shareholders, who along with other executives and managers who are in the Leger Profit Sharing Program (PSP), share a long successful engagement with Leger. These include Anne-Marie Marois who joined in November 1990, now COO; Jean-Sebastien Simard, now Executive VP (EVP) Leger Opinion Polls who joined in 1993; Christian Bourque, now EVP and Senior Partner who joined in May 1999; Dave Scholz, now EVP who joined in October 2000; Sandrine Lepinay, now EVP who joined in April 2002; Benoit Belanger, now CFO who joined in 2003; Steve Perrone, Chief Technical Officer who joined in January 2005; Simon Jaworski, President US and EVP who joined in January 2008; Ian Large, now EVP Western Canada who joined in January 2010; Sandi Sparkman, now EVP Client Solutions who joined EVP in September 2013; and more recently Steve Massop, EVP Vancouver who joined with the 2021 acquisitions. The strength of staff relations is also shown by the low 2.5% staff turnover amongst both their 265 full time professionals and their 335 permanent part time staff.

Fifth, as an SME with limited resources, be practical about acquisitions. Jean-Marc calls this "2-2-2 Rules":

"You will have 2 x less revenue than expected. You will have 2 x less profit than expected. And it will take 2 x longer to achieve your goals. If it is still valuable, then you go ahead."

Sixth, in thinking about entrance to the US, recognize it is a different market: more competitive, more specialized, more tech-oriented and larger competitors. This has, and will impact the way Leger deals with US expansion. They are learning about the market from their activity in their current Philadelphia base.

Seventh, competition changes. In Canada many previous Canadian competitors have either gone out of business or sold. Leger is probably the second largest research company in Canada, but has to compete with global players like Ipsos and SIS; mid-sized Canadian operations like Environics and the Research Strategy Group, and many small players. The key here is meeting client needs better and in a differentiated way, and that comes from the people and the technology.

Eighth, the importance of staying close to clients and understanding their changing needs for data and analysis, and the speed with which this is required in contemporary decision making. Leger has many long-term clients such as GSK (Glaxo Smith-Kline), L'Oreal, Nestle (Nespresso), Pfizer, Quebecor, Telus and Welcome Pharma, and with acquisition and offerings in analytics now many more. As Jean-Marc describes it:

"We have 'zipper' client relationships. We each have multi-relations with clients at different levels and in different departments, which helps manage changes in client personnel."

Ninth, be active in promotion and marketing communications. For Leger it has a B2B focus. Leger has consistently used its polling results to gain media coverage, be these political or more frequently, issue-based social attitudes. In addition, they run conferences and seminars regarding these issues targeting businesses, governments, academics and the NGO sectors. For example, in April each year, they publish the results of their Corporate Reputation Study and hold a session for guests: this has been running for 25 years. In addition, they publish papers, articles and books, the latest book being *"Cracking the Quebec Code in 45 Minutes – the 7 Keys to succeed in Quebec"* in April 2022.

Tenth, learn from everyone globally. Jean-Marc and the Leger organization have been involved and active in a number of global organizations. In 2010, Jean-Marc became founding President of WIN, a worldwide association of polling firms that includes 75 major independent research firms from 73 countries. Through this engagement they have developed strong relationships with the best research companies across the world to their mutual benefit.

In summary, to quote Jean-Marc:

"We have succeeded because we transform ourselves every day."

The Future,

Alan: *"So you are constantly thinking about the future?"*

Jean-Marc: *"Oh yes, that's my job. To be sure that for our clients we are there in the right place, with the right tools and the right people for the future."*

Like many organizations, labour and talent shortages and increasing salary costs confront Leger. However, because of the low staff turnover and good staff relations this is being handled well by their HR Director, Veronique Marois-Lippinghof, another long–term (November 2010) senior executive, and their hiring and skills upgrade programs. Jean-Marc, along with others, see data security and data privacy as a big issue. They now have a full-time lawyer on staff and are working to increase data confidentiality but without it resulting in bureaucratic excesses. Leger has goals to become a $100 million company, and go to the stock market, probably with more acquisition/expansion in the US and/or internationally. To do this, Jean-Marc recognizes that the ability to reach this critical mass is driven by the need to have:

"Happy and successful employees, delivering a best-in-class quality at an increasing speed and depth of analysis."

Interview March 25th 2022.

4

SME MARKETING CHALLENGE #4: COMMUNICATE, COMMUNICATE, COMMUNICATE!

"It's not what you sell that matters as much as how you sell it."

Brian Halligan, 1967 – date. American, CEO and Co-Founder HubSpot.

As indicated earlier, evidence suggests that Canadian SMEs underinvest in marketing in general and marketing communications in particular– the 'P" in the Promotion entry in the 'Marketing Mix 10'.

So, first let's deal with the range of communications options. Although the list of planned message media is long, communication gets to the target groups by even wider sources:

Planned(controlled) messages:

Media advertising (TV, radio, newspaper, magazine, outdoor billboards), web site(s), sales promotion including product sampling and discounting, marketing public relations, direct marketing, personal selling, point of purchase and merchandising materials, packaging, specialties, events, sponsorship marketing, licensing, customer service, internal marketing, on-line communications (e blasts etc.), Google, paid social media like Facebook, Linked-In, You Tube, WhatsApp, Instagram, WeChat, Twitter, Tik Tok, Snapchat, Pinterest, Reddit.

Unplanned (uncontrolled) messages:

Employee gossip and behavior in-person and online, media investigation, government investigations, consumer group investigations, chat groups, on-line guerrilla sites, blogs, citizen journalism, informal social media.

Too often Unconsidered:

Facility function and design (especially retail but also offices), services offered, distribution channels, product design, product performance, price.

The point is that in the contemporary world all an SME's activities are part of its communications to customers, prospects, staff, competitors, regulators and influencers which is why its impacts should be considered and planned.

Currently in Canada, about 60% of paid media goes through the internet, about 20% goes through various TV channels (network and specialist); about 8% in radio; 6% in newspapers; 4% in outdoor; and around 1% in magazines.

Data regarding spending in Canada by SMEs is limited but as indicated earlier, US organizations spend at levels between 33% and 50% higher per revenue than Canadians. This Advertising/Sales (A/S) ratio in the US ranges from around 2% for Tech. products, almost 3% for B2B businesses, and up to as high as 17-20% for consumer products such as cosmetics and toiletries.

In general terms in Canada, the highest spending categories are Retail, Automotive, Financial Institutions, Food and Beverage and Pharmaceutical/Cosmetics and Toiletries. Pre-pandemic Entertainment and Travel & Tourism were also high, but reduced dramatically during the 2020 – 2022 pandemic.

In terms of paid and planned media, the following elements should be considered. You can't afford to be everywhere, therefore Tools 4.1. and 4.2. should help guide you.

SME Marketing Challenge Tool #4.1. Marketing Communications: Media Choice Criteria

- Define the target group as fully as possible.

- What media does your target group see/hear, and engage. Get data from surveys and reliable sources, but also what do your best customers tell you?

- What is the objective of your communication? Announcement? Gain leads? Provide ongoing brand communication? Most marketing communication should be continuous yet updated, other than special short-term communications efforts. Many SMEs run their marketing communications for far too brief a period of time to achieve objectives like awareness, purchase consideration and brand trust.

- How will you integrate this activity into your sales activity?

- How will you measure the success or failure based on your objectives? What (reliable) data does the media provider have to show success in similar business categories to yours?

- How will you brief your own staff about the message and the media and what is their role in getting the message out?

- As many in our smaller SMEs have done (Diabetes Care Community, Hatley and Mother Raw), hire a specialist marketing communications agency to help develop your plan.

The Creative message also has some criteria to be followed in order to ensure your messages are designed to achieve the responses you want from the target group.

SME Marketing Challenge Tool #4.2. Marketing Communications: Creative Briefing Criteria

1. Define the target group as fully as possible.
- What is the objective of your communication? What target group attitudes and /or behaviors do you want to change/encourage.

2. Prior campaigns
- What prior messages have been sent and what do we know about the response to them. Should we be building on these or taking a 'fresh' approach.

3. Integrate Communication:
- What messages in other media are being sent – how does this message integrate with those.

4. Competitors:
- Who are the major competitors? Is there loyalty? How much variation is there in brand purchase? How much is online or in person?

5. Brand Insight
*   Summarize what is currently in the target group's mind (positive or negative) about their needs and the brand relative to alternatives - current and desired.

6. Brand Positioning – Intended
*   As indicated in chapter 2, brand positioning is the way you intend your target group to "see" the brand and its benefits: a combination of awareness and impressions in both memory and immediate experience that set it apart and better than its competition. There are three ways you can use to achieve a favourable positioning:

*   Notice: from the senses (sight, sound, smell, taste, touch) what do you want your target group to experience about the brand's product and its presentation compared to its competition.

*   Believe: from thought and analysis what do you want your target group to believe about the brand compared to its competition.

*   Feel: emotionally what do you want your target group to feel about the brand compared to its competition.

*   The core benefit: Which of the preceding is the focus of needs met and benefits supplied to give a meaningful and differentiated position versus competition and avoid category generic appeals.

7. Brand Voice and Personality
*   If your brand came to life, who would it be: what kind of a personality? Why would you make them a friend or close colleague? Is it their knowledge, skills, thriftiness, great taste, looks, fashion sense, health, sportiness, personality (warmth, manner, exuberance, quiet confidence, uncomplicated, joyful etc.)?

8. Brand Image
*   Summarize in one phrase the singular impression/image you want your target group to have about your brand: must be researchable

9. Brand Essence
*   The distillation of the brand's positioning, promise and image into one clear thought that sets it apart from competition (e.g., Pepsi Challenge: Pepsi tastes better than Coke which is why you should buy it for your family; BMW: performance based

German engineering; Apple: ease of use and the most widespread acceptance.

10. Timetable for development and feedback.
* Once again consider hiring a creative services agency – but make sure they have an understanding of strategy and the target group.

SMEs can benefit enormously from better planned and more extensive marketing communications. There are many great examples in the SME Stories, but particularly the Harry Rosen and Sleep Country stories. There is much expertise around to help. Many on the roster of the AMA Toronto chapter have world class expertise in these disciplines. Use them!

SME Story #4.1 Harry Rosen Inc.

A small company, growing to medium and now large size, Harry Rosen Inc. is the leading Canadian retail chain and online site for luxury men's clothing and recently, men's grooming products.

Founded by Harry Rosen in 1954, as a single 500 square foot (46 m2) store in Cabbagetown, Toronto, they now operate 17 x Harry Rosen stores across Canada, 3 x "The Outlet by Harry Rosen" stores and "shopfinalcut.com". They have 1,200 employees and revenues of around $211 million. Growth came by: offering high quality custom tailoring and collections of high-end labels like Tom Ford, Brunello Cucinelli, Zegna, Emporio Armani and Hugo Boss; expansion of outlets in Toronto (including a 50,000 sq.ft. store on Bloor Street) and Mississauga, Ottawa, Montreal, Winnipeg, Edmonton, Calgary and Vancouver; extensive employee training and commitment early on to award-winning and contemporary marketing communications.

Interview with Trinh Tham, Chief Marketing Officer/ EVP Marketing and E- Commerce; and an AMA Toronto Marketing Networking Group online presentation by Ian Rosen, President and COO, and Trihn Tham.

The success of Harry Rosen from its founding on February 4th 1954 in a small made-to-measure store on Parliament Street in Toronto to the top men's clothing store chain and a heritage brand in Canada is a marketing story par excellence. It has been built on:

- A clear vision and mission: *"Help men feel confident by looking and feeling their best."* - A deep understanding of the customer and their clothing needs and desires.

- Attention to staff training and motivation as part of the Harry Rosen community to build trust with their clients.

- An abiding focus on the finest quality and cut of the clothing.

- A pricing strategy that matched the brand positioning to be the best, indeed luxury, of what was available.

- A history of expanding distribution through growth in retail stores and, in the last 10 years, meeting client needs both online and offline.

- Constant activity to promote the brand in advertising and other marketing communications media with style, sense of humour and a strong Canadian presence.

- Consistency and a strong sense of brand values.

- Keeping their business technology constantly updated and especially links between suppliers, the company and the customer.

The Management Team.

Guiding and implementing this approach have been the Rosen family and experienced professionals. In November 2019, Trinh Tham joined as Chief Marketing Officer/EVP Marketing and E-Commerce, after a stellar career in brand marketing, and particularly Canadian brand marketing, with Loblaws, Bell Media Tim Hortons and Sobeys. She is now working in the executive team with Larry Rosen, Harry's son and the CEO, Ian Rosen, previously Executive VP Digital and Strategy now the President and COO, and others like Alan Whitfield, VP Store Operations and Carolyn Tyrie, Chief HR Executive who have worked with Rosen for over 25 years.

Customer Centricity and their Clothing Needs.

As Ian Rosen says:

"We were born and bred just thinking about the customer. We were built as a word-of-mouth engine."

Trinh reflects:

"As Harry says, he has built the business one customer at a time. From the very beginning the business had a purpose, to help men feel confident by looking their best. The evolution of the business is that and being true to who we are. With that, we have always been focused on quality, craftsmanship and customization."

The Harry Rosen target group was across age but appealed to men whose work, position or taste led them to investigate high quality, well designed and fitting clothing. Mostly suits, jackets and pants in the early days but now much more leisure and casual attire. Harry Rosen was early to bring in fine menswear labels from Europe and then North America: names like Brioni, Hugo Boss, Burberry, Canali, Dolce & Gabbana, Emporio Armani, Kiton, Zegna and Tom Ford as well as some great Canadian designers. A mark of the Harry Rosen business culture was, and is, the closeness of relationships with these and other suppliers and partners. It was why, even before the pandemic, the 'casualization' of clothing was being responded to throughout Harry Rosen's operations with items like running attire.

The casualization of apparel trend accelerated through the pandemic, as Ian comments:

"Everyone went to 'Zoomwear', so we rallied everyone around the idea being great at casualwear, but staying true to helping people look and feel their best no matter if they are wearing a suit or a sweater."

This emphasis on both formal and casual was accomplished most successfully and remains a key part of their product offerings to this day.

Competition comes mostly from department stores, specialty retailers and these days, online sites, and particularly international sites. The shift to casual clothing has meant the need to sell more items than the previous mainly suit business to make the revenues. Wedding outfits, though, remain an important part of the business. Now, Harry Rosen is not only about clothing. In early 2021 they launched their personal care brand marketplace. As Ian Rosen said at the time:

"Harry Rosen has been all about helping men feel their most confident, so that they do their best. Nothing in that statement starts or stops with clothing."

They launched a multi-brand men's grooming dropship platform with some 400 products, 25% of which are Canadian. An early addition were the products (and advice) of "Educated Beards", a Canadian company founded in 2017 to promote products for healthy hair, eliminate itching, irritation, beardruff, and give the user greater control of their beard.

Employee Culture

Staff, particularly the style advisers, receive extensive training on the nuances of designer fashion including the art of "clothesmanship", determining the right garment for a man's body shape. Staff are also provided training on how to manage client lists, how to assess client needs, how men shop in general, and how to build and maintain long term relationships with clients. As Trinh comments:

"With luxury clothing you are creating a relationship with your customer; you are having real conversations; you have a unique relationship with your style advisor that can be quite personal. We thriver on how to help customers feel as special as possible."

Their stores have a large number of long-term employees. According to Trinh:

"Many employees and clients became "influencers" long before the digital media introduced that terminology".

The 'brand refresh' launched in August 2020 focused staff on some key principles that reflect both the traditional values and the new environment. Ian outlines these as:

"– be customer centric: always keep the customer in mind across the various functional areas, whether we are in marketing, IT, buying or other roles;

– measure twice, cut once', which harks back to that we wouldn't rush an alteration and put you in something that doesn't fit;

– being a leader, we dress and outfit leaders so we are all leaders;

– being very welcoming and inclusive when you walk into our store and shop with us.

We evaluate our team at Harry Rosen against those values."

This focus on every role in their employee culture and by a *"bottom - up movement empowered by executives, we are building a more diverse and equitable work and customer environment"*. This has helped them move through the pandemic and prepare for a more online, casual, and youthfully diverse Canadian market.

Distribution Expansion

Expansion has been continuous since their founding on Parliament Street in Toronto in 1954, which had been opened with a $500 down payment. All future growth was funded through earnings. In Toronto, the first expansion came in 1961 with the move to Richmond Street in the Financial District, and then in 1987 to the 32,000 sq ft three level store on the fashionable Bloor Street, and in 2008 the expansion of this store to five floors (50,000 sq ft). National expansion started in 1981 when they opened in Edmonton at West Edmonton Mall. Since then, they have opened four more stores in Toronto plus Mississauga, Ottawa, Montreal, Winnipeg, Calgary and Vancouver. Work on digital selling started early enabled by their detailed customer records and high levels of customer satisfaction. This has been accelerated by the work of Ian Rosen and Trinh and the pandemic impacts which have caused a tripling of online sales. The recently launched online site "shopfinalcut. com" is a further development to respond to this trend.

Marketing Communications

All Harry Rosen marketing communication builds off the central vision and mission *"to help men feel confident by looking and feeling their best"*. As Ian Rosen now says:

"The brand messaging that we put out isn't about 'buy, buy, buy', it's about 'help accomplish what you want to look like'. It's always been laddering up to the idea of helping the customer."

Much of Harry Rosen's success can be attributed to early advertising helped by Stann Burkhoff, a customer of his: they developed the early "Ask Harry" newspaper advertising campaign. This posed clothing questions like one for trousers: *"How wide should cuffs be? The knee?"* and then the response: *"Ask Harry."* The concept continues through its site "Clothing Advisor" with questions like: *"How do I break out of my suit and tie rut, and get me more creative with my wardrobe?"*

Harry's humour would occasionally appear in their advertising. During one economic slump he ran ads with the line: *"The Not So Good for Us, But Good for You Sale"*

They have continued strong advertising activity with some famous campaigns, including the award-winning Canadian newspaper campaign *"Whatever Suits You"* from 1996 onwards which featured Canadian celebrities such as David Cronenberg, Norman Jewison, Christopher Plummer, Remy Shand and Rick Mercer. They also ran ads featuring other customers. In 2000 they launched a $3 million newspaper campaign aimed at younger audiences and the increasing trend towards more casual office wear. As the advertising tag line indicated: *"You'll face a number of dilemmas in a day, what to wear shouldn't be one of them."* As Larry Rosen commented at the launch of the campaign:

"We can't help with your daily life, but what we can do is make sure you're dressed appropriately for any occasion."

In 2018, TV was added to their marketing communications mix and an increasing online presence.

In August 2020, when the brand refresh was implemented, it maintains the original vision and mission but, as Trihn indicates, articulates values to also be reflected in their external branding:

"Four key values: Leadership. Passion. Creativity. Inclusivity."

The brand workshop that Trinh led sought input from everyone, not just marketing, and its goal was to maintain core values but address contemporary demographic, socio-cultural and style issues.

The website was significantly updated, and the new *"Set the Tone"* brand campaign was launched. Set the tone for whatever is in the customer's day or life: professionally or personally, as well as being socially and environmentally conscious.

"With the pandemic effect, so much has changed. We are much more aware of social issues. You can't ignore the impact a brand has socially, and so 'Set the Tone' also speaks to this aspect."

Featuring Canadian actor Emmanuel Kabongo, 'Set the Tone' is about looking and feeling the best no matter what the customer has to tackle in their day. Recently they did a collaboration with Masai Ujiri, the

President of the Toronto Raptors, and beloved Canadian designer Patrick Assaraf. The capsule collection, now in its second season, centres around Masai on the "#That's Humanity" movement that has been growing to support diversity and inclusivity.

"We worked with him on a collection that really centered around what humanity means for Masai personally and to encourage everyone to think about what it means for youth. He is someone who exemplifies leadership, passion, creativity and community. We are continuing to look to express our brand through supporting leaders and role models."

The online world and the omnichannel approach with their customers in the retail stores means much better targeting and responsiveness to their messaging. There will be online, content and more seasonal campaigns to allow greater flexibility, an example being the current "Harry Rosen Spring/Summer 2022 Luxury Collection". As Trinh says:

"To be in market quickly with relevant topics for our customers."

This also allows better targeting by age, ethnicity, region and clothing preference.

Harry Rosen has successfully used marketing communication as a continuous brand and business building activity. It has kept current with fashion trends (a broad choice of casual clothing); demographic trends (immigration numbers and backgrounds, and diversity and inclusion issues), media trends and the evolving in-store and digital channels. As Trinh comments:

"Harry always injected humour into things and the organization has always been willing to take risks based on attention to our culture and demographic changes; with the messaging and with some of the product lines. Rosen has always been great at bringing new brands in and exploring new ideas for our customers. Harry really was a true visionary."

Constant Improvements in Business Technology

Since late 2019 and led by Ian Rosen, the company has been innovating its business processes to provide quicker, more flexible and better service to its customers. Using the services of "Convictional", a B2B software company, they went "headless": a software architecture model that uses different, specialized software for their backend and their frontend. Decoupling backend systems from frontend website enables them to meet customer demand but at greater speed. It also enables Harry Rosen to provide great service for their brand partners on the Harry Rosen website and thereby continue strong customer relations. Second, they have a "dropship" process that allows website orders to be sourced directly from supplier production without having to store inventory. This was instrumental in establishing the men's grooming platform referred to earlier.

Conclusion

Through three generations of the Rosen family and the addition of highly talented professionals, Harry Rosen maintains its abiding orientation to its vision and mission and most importantly quality, customer, staff and supplier care but still innovates and meets the needs of a changing business, technological and social environment.

Lessons for SMEs:

- Apply all the marketing principles with close input and relationships with the customer

- Be agile and courageous in addressing these.

- Tell people about your brand with a tone and manner appropriate to the audience and your brand purpose and values.

- Work as an integrated management team.

- Build a positive employee culture by listening to, involving and valuing all roles and their inputs.

- While not losing sight of your vision, mission and objectives, stay current with changes in demographics, tastes, culture, and technology.

Interview with Trinh Tham February 16th 2022.

AMA Toronto Marketing Networking Group online presentation by Ian Rosen and Trinh Tham February 23rd 2022.

SME Story 4.2. Sleep Country Canada Holdings Inc.

A small, then medium and now large size public company retailing mattresses and accessories for the bedroom across Canada.

Launched in 1994 in Vancouver by three partners, Christine Magee, Stephen K. Gunn, and Gordon Lownds, Sleep Country now has 286 stores, and 20 distribution centres with 1,600 employees and revenues of over $920 million. Following an IPO in 2015, Sleep Country continues to thrive from its Toronto headquarters. In 2018, they acquired Endy Sleep, an innovative manufacturer and online seller of high quality mattresses, and in late 2021 Hush Blankets Inc., an online supplier of high quality blankets.

Interview with Christine Magee, Co-Founder and Executive Co-Chair.

Background

In the early 1980s, three highly motivated individuals met and saw an opportunity for a more consumer–oriented approach for retailing mattresses and bedding accessories. Christine Magee had spent 13 years in banking with the Continental Bank and the National Bank. During her time there she met her future business partners, Stephen Gunn and Gordon Lownds who had a private equity company called Kennick Capital. In the late 1980s Kennick had completed a management buyout of Simmons Canada from its parent company Simmons US, a well-known brand manufacturer of mattresses. Based on their knowledge of the mattress and bedding industry, they were struck by its manufacturing rather than consumer perspective. Manufacturers were well-branded, serving a highly competitive marketplace. About 50% share sold through department stores like The Bay, Sears, Eaton's, and a handful of national furniture/appliance stores like The Brick. The balance was highly fragmented across a host of smaller regional or one- off stores. As Christine comments:

"No national footprint retailer. No retail operations were providing the quality of customer experience that this important category deserved. It was a manufacturing play."

Based on this, Stephen and Gordon invited Christine to join them in a retail mattress startup. She did.

They developed a business plan based on their knowledge of the Canadian landscape including market data and qualitative and anecdotal experiences of family, friends and colleagues when purchasing a mattress.

"The retail environment was very hard sell, very pushy. Products were commoditized and at retail it lacked any kind of customer experience or attention to build loyalty. But there were fundamentals that made this category appealing. It was a needs-based purchase: mattresses are replaced on average every 10-12 years contributing to a steady, stable recurring demand. There was a strong just-in-time manufacturing supply base; a growing population and an increasing focus on sleep and health. All of which made this category attractive with a timely opportunity given the lack of service and attention to the customer needs."

To validate their business plan and concept, they looked for some successful US models. They were introduced to a company called Sleep Country USA, then operating 15 stores on the west coast in Washington State:

"They were doing amazing things on the west coast; they had been in business for nearly four years and had already built tremendous market share."

They gained direct input from the owners at Sleep Country USA:

"How they approached the category, their marketing, their in-store experience, their store design; their ERP system and more."

As they went through the ideation and planning stages, they decided on the name and bought the trade mark, Sleep Country Canada from the US company, and even the Sleep Country USA jingle. They further leveraged the US operations in their initial sales training and in-store merchandizing.

Start Up

Gordon and Christine and their families then moved out to Vancouver to set up the company. Sleep Country Canada launched in Vancouver in October 1994 with 4 stores, and then opened almost one per month until they had 10 stores in Greater Vancouver and 2 on Vancouver

Island in the first year of operation. The format of the stores was for a size of 5,000 – 7,000 square feet and 2 – 4 sales associates per store: a model they took across Canada. They recognized that they should concentrate and get to "critical mass" quickly. This had advantages in distribution and delivery as well as advertising. Vancouver was ideal: it was close to Sleep Country USA for training and communication (including a little "halo" effect from their advertising), and:

"With a population of some 1.8 million it was manageable. We could establish a central warehouse; populate the city with stores; blanket the city with advertising and therefore test the hypothesis of how we would go to market."

Their vision was not just to sell mattresses but:

"To help customers get a great night's sleep."

Their initial target group was women 25 – 54, then broadening to all adults. Stores were to be conveniently located in major population areas to offer superior customer access, advice and service. They made the decision that someone from the company should appear in the advertising to personalize the brand and help communicate the company's values and commitment to service. Based on the female skew of their target group, of the three partners they decided Christine should be the spokesperson.

"The idea of having a female President as the spokesperson resonated with our customers. We benefited from increased press and favorable coverage which really helped jumpstart our company."

Intensive advertising in primarily radio (60%) and some TV (40%) drove the message along with in-store material. They always had two styles of ads: those that were promotional and those about their vision and mission around the importance of sleep and the values they stood for in the community. The brand goal was trust, credibility and the positive sales, delivery and customer experience they offered.

Getting broadly known and available was key to their strategy, to:

"– build top of mind awareness;

– build a consultative and friendly in-store culture through staff and store design;

– build timely, friendly and reliable home delivery."

For the next several years, it was *"24/7"* for the owners and their growing business team. Finding staff and training them was a big challenge even with the help of the US company. They had to be trained in a much more consultative approach of guiding people to get a better night's sleep, not just product features and price.

"We wanted the customer to have an enjoyable experience, from our initial greeting, through our consultative process in which we ask a customer about their sleep needs, their budget, and then lead them through the process to help each customer make the decision that is right for them."

Building that in-store staff ("Sales Associate") culture came through a 5-week training program (classroom, manufacturer briefing, in-store role playing). Home delivery was of equal focus: providing a professional, comfortable uniformed delivery experience with a guaranteed 3-hour delivery window, set-up and offer to take away the old mattress:

"It is the last face our customer sees. We need it to be exceptional."

They kept investing in the business, especially in the advertising and it was becoming clear that the business strategy and model was working. By the Fall of 1995 they were close to break- even, so they started planning their next move. In February 1996, they opened 10 stores in Toronto.

Expansion

The multi-store opening approach had been proved in Vancouver, so based on siting about one store per 130,000 population, in convenient, highly visible and delivery-convenient distance (about 15 kilometers) from customer's homes, they opened Toronto. In 1996/1997, they opened 19 stores in Toronto and within two years had grown to 32 stores. In Fall 1997, they opened 4 stores in Calgary bringing the store count to 50 stores within 3 years of their initial launch. Sleep Country continued expanding across Canada with the exception of Quebec where they recognized they needed a different approach. By 2001, they had 72 stores in six regional markets and in those markets about a 40% brand share.

They pushed themselves only adding overhead in a step function when absolutely needed. The business at this time was still primarily mattresses from established manufactures like Simmons, Sealy, Serta and Kingsdown, but with the growth of Sleep Country their negotiating position strengthened and they built closer and more collaborative relationships in areas like joint merchandising. The commitment to advertising continued and its slogan "why buy a mattress anywhere else" remains one of the most recognized in Canada.

In 2003, Sleep Country Canada converted into an income trust and raised nearly $130 million in its IPO: this enabled them to make their next moves. In January 2006, they purchased Dormez-vous Sleep Centres Inc. with its 5 stores in Montreal. They basically allowed the local management to continue but added Sleep Country's strengths. Stewart Schaefer, now President and CEO of Sleep Country Canada, came on board at that time as the President of "Dormez-vous?", the company he had founded. They now have 61 stores in Quebec. Also, in 2006 they acquired Sleep America with stores in Arizona, mostly in Phoenix and Tucson. While successful despite stiff competition, more opportunities in Canada loomed so in 2013 they sold the US business.

In 2010, they started to expand their product ranges from primarily mattresses and box springs by adding accessories: bed frames, box springs, headboards, bed linens and pillows which now account for about 20% of their business.

In 2015, their corporate status changed as they went public with an IPO on the Toronto Stock Exchange (symbol:" ZZZ") that raised $300 million. This was to provide liquidity and to help their exit from their initial funding arrangements.

In 2017, they launched their e-commerce site to enable ordering and direct delivery of accessory items and then mattresses. Sleep Country Canada added to its mattress suppliers in 2019 with an agreement with the innovative UK company Simba Sleep. This subsequently transformed into a partnership with Simba Sleep Canada in October 2021.

In November 2018, they purchased Endy Sleep for $89 million. Endy was a Canadian direct to home mattress manufacturer. They had launched in 2015 and within 3 years had achieved $20+ million in sales and were already profitable. Competitors like Casper from New York sold mattresses both online and through retailers so the additional distribution of Endy mattresses to Sleep Country stores added enormously to the potential.

"To some extent they were serving customers that weren't coming into Sleep Country retail: a generation that chose not to come into a store because they could buy online."

This acquisition also helped Sleep Country develop its omnichannel approach to its customers, enabling them to track customer demographics and preferences and offering them both retail and online buying convenience for both mattresses and accessories.

In late 2021, they continued to expand their sleep accessories business with the acquisition of Hush Blankets Inc, an online supplier of high quality bed blankets.

Management Development

In recent years the founders, Stephen Gunn and Christine Magee, have taken a more governance role as Co-Chairs of the Board. Gordon Lownds left active engagement with Sleep Country in 1998, and Stephen Gunn retired as Co-Chair in May 2019. The 18–person senior leadership team, known as the Central Support Group, runs the company. This team combines members with deep experience with the company and new members with new and necessary skills as the company transforms to retail's changing environment and omnichannel platform. The group includes Stewart Schaefer, since January 1st 2022 the President/CEO, who had joined them in 2006 as President of the newly acquired "Dormez-vous?" which he had founded in 1994. Craig De Pratto, their Chief Financial Officer, joined in 2019; and David Howcroft, their Chief Sales Officer, has been with them since 1996. Endy is run by the President and General Manager Alexandra Voyevodina-Wang, who took over from the co-founder Mike Gettis.

Future Developments

Sleep Country will not sleep: in fiscal year 2021 revenues grew 21.4% to $920.2 million. E-commerce revenues were 24% of the total. For the future as Christine comments:

"We have a Canadian footprint and we continue to build our sleep ecosystem through our expanded product line-up and e-Commerce platforms, including expanding into new marketplace concepts with Walmart and Loblaws; partnerships with innovative mattress companies like Simba, Casper and Purple; we have Endy and Hush. We are dedicated to improving the lives of our customers through promoting the power of sleep and will continue to work hard to provide exceptional customer service and provide the best assortment of mattresses and sleep products for people to buy now and into the future."

Lessons for SMEs.

- Build strategy and operations around a customer driven vision and mission: Sleep Country was always about *"to help customers get a great night's sleep"*: not just to sell mattresses. To this day this thought remains:

  *"Our **Purpose** is to transform lives by awakening Canadians to the power of sleep.*

  *Our **Vision** is to champion sleep as the key to healthier, happier lives and to help everyone achieve better tomorrows through better tonights."*

- Plan, review, learn and adapt in a formal planning process.

- Keep current with customer demographic and socio-cultural changes: attitudes and behaviors: anticipate. Talk to the customer – constantly.

- Build a strong customer experience while buying: encourage loyalty and positive reference by understanding not only the product but its role in the customer's lives.

- Build a strong staff culture by training, incentive, multicultural inclusion and example.

  "The key role for the leadership team is to support the folks that are dealing with the customer on the front line, in-store, home delivery, customer service, and to empower them to do whatever it takes to deliver good service."

- Ensure easy availability and accessibility to purchase.

- Promote actively and continuously: do not start then stop or underspend:

  "Be top of mind and in your face."

- Be bold: make your plan and go for it: multiple store openings funding substantial advertising activity attests to this thinking.

- Be bold in the funding strategy.

Christine Magee has a great view of the role of marketing, well worth repeating:

"Marketing and advertising to me are all about execution. Advertising is one part of your brand building – really critical in the promises you set out for the marketplace to expect and the values you believe in. The reality of that brand is then what the customer experiences when they come in and purchase. And in the delivery, the last face the customer sees. They are our ambassadors. For the past 28 years our whole focus is to keep the business very simple and focus on those three things: in-store, home delivery and our marketing to live up to the promises. We want you to have the best night's sleep and the best service."

Interview: Christine Magee, February 28th 2022.

5

SME MARKETING CHALLENGE #5: STAFF AND CUSTOMERS ARE "TWO SIDES OF THE SAME COIN"

"The way you treat your employees is the way they will treat your customers."

Sir Richard Branson, 1950 – date. British, Founder, Virgin Group.

In the pandemic and post pandemic periods the importance of all staff including the critical front-line staff became more and more apparent in all organizations. This has always been the People 'P' in the Marketing Mix but in a service majority economy (65% of GDP) and in the post–pandemic world, they are more important than ever. This is especially true of SMEs whose staff resources tend to be smaller. Here the staff tend to have greater responsibility and have important external friendship groups where they talk about work and other issues that impact the SME brand. In my book "Mentorship Matters:

Now More than Ever" I recommended the book "Humanocracy" by Gary Hamel and Michele Zanini. Their view on how business organization structures must evolve is directly pertinent: here's how they see a 'Humanocracy':

- Influence is earned from peers.

- Strategy is open to firm-wide conversation.

- Resources are allocated by market mechanism.

- Innovation is everyone's job.

- Coordination comes from collaboration.

- Roles built round individual skills.

- Teams divide up work.

- Control comes from transparency and peers.

- Staff groups compete against external vendors.

- Individuals compete to add value.

- Critical trade-offs are optimized locally.

- Units are responsible for local P&Ls.

- Compensation correlates with impact.

- Employees have significant financial upside.

- Self-managing teams/individuals.

Staff engagement - all staff - is critical for marketing for a number of reasons:

- Recruitment: getting a reputation that the organization is a great place to work so as to attract the best staff.

- Employee motivation and retention to reduce cost of staff turnover and the disruption that comes from this plus demotivated staff.

- Customer engagement so that they are well served and treated by staff to enhance the relationship with the SME brand,

As such, employee knowledge and commitment must not only relate to product knowledge or their particular role, but to what the brand is and the values of the organization in what service it provides its customer. This has been particularly true of our SME Stories from Nature's Path, Umbra and others in this book. It needs to be reflected in the strategic orientation of senior management and in all staff communications and training.

Building a strong internal community and a strong brand through its people comes from:

- The collective knowledge and skill of employees and how they are compensated.

- The organization's purpose and values.

- The relationships with customers.

- The commitment to innovation and improvement by all.

Internal Communications must therefore build a good knowledge and understanding of the SME brand(s) and its marketing activity. It can do this through:

- Brand Training

- Brand book as a reference

- Brand value statement

- Brand stories and role models

- Internal central, cascaded and interactive communications must also be aligned around the brand themes.

With social media now so critical in all our lives, having a motivated and loyal staff and having them talk about it in their personal lives is an essential for success.

Looking after your people is also a critical element in delivering great customer service whether you are selling products or services. Increasingly the quality of the purchase and user experience is a critical differentiating element in brand purchase. Poor customer service can lose business, but the reasons are often misunderstood.

In ground-breaking research in 1985 and consistently confirmed since, three researchers (Parasuraman, Zeithamel and Berry) outlined where service gaps occurred. They were as follows:

SME Marketing Challenge Tool #5: Service Gap Sources and Solutions

Gap #1: Between what management perception of customers' service expectations are versus what the customers' expected level of service is.

- Too often management sets policies without finding out what is important to the customer. Issues of speed, quality, personal contact, level of explanation are often conflicting but need to be understood.

- Resolution: better research with customers.

Gap #2: Between Service Quality Specifications for staff and management's researched understanding of what customers expect.

- Too often even when management through its research has a good understanding of customer expectations, when written as specifications they are inaccurate or incomplete and can be misunderstood or ignored by staff.

- Resolution: work with front line staff to review the research and delivery.

Gap #3: Between Service Quality Specifications and actual Service Delivery.

- Many people assume that this is the major service problem: that it is the failure of individual staff members to perform to expectation. The research indicates this is not the case. In fact, the problems are pretty evenly spread across the five gaps. However, Gap #3 does exist. But again, there is misunderstanding as to the reasons. The biggest reason is that insufficient resources in time, training and money are allocated to enable the specifications to be delivered well.

- Resolution: ensure that when the customer research is being reviewed and specifications set, that sufficient resources in time, training and money are allocated.

Gap #4: Between Service Delivery and Customer Communication.

- There is a tendency in customer-oriented marketing communications for exaggerated promises as to service delivery and satisfaction. While marketing communications will always *"accentuate the positive and eliminate the negative"* (song written by Harold Arlen and Johnny Mercer in 1944), there is a point where the claims can become legally misleading, or set expectations beyond what can be realistically accomplished. This sets up unrealistic expectations and results in a higher level of dissatisfaction than if the claims had not been made. A potentially severe damage to the brand reputation and business.

- Resolution: while marketing communications does need to be positive, practitioners must be sure to avoid exaggeration and setting unrealistic service expectations.

Gap #5: Between the Perceived Service Delivery and the Customer Expectations.

- This is a complex issue because sometimes, it deals with irrational or highly unrealistic expectations by the customer that cannot be delivered. Some extreme examples to make the point: when going to healthcare providers for treatment for serious and life-threatening problems, the expectation of 'fix it' is often impossible. A friend who was an eminent plastic surgeon was often faced with expectations that relatively minor surgery would make the patient beautiful and highly attractive, when often the surgery would only make minor modifications.

- In the everyday commercial world, we often want things of high quality, immediate delivery and low cost when we really know there have to be trade-offs.

- Resolution: explanation of what is possible and the trade offs so that the customer understands more about what can be accomplished. It won't always work, but to most people an understanding of the issues will help acceptance of realistic service expectations.

A better understanding of where the service gaps might be in your SME will help not only address increasing expectations for improved service but also save money being wasted in unnecessary or potentially more expensive features.

SME Story 5.1. Hatley and Little Blue House

A successful medium sized family enterprise doing business internationally and successfully pivoting through the Covid-19 pandemic.

Trading under its Hatley corporate brand and its original Little Blue House brand, this family-owned company of around $65 million gross sales and 320 employees sells children's clothing, casual women's clothing, and a range of gift items that are mostly clothing, through 4,000 outlets in Canada, the US, the UK and other countries. They sell through wholesalers into retailers, their own retail outlets, and online through their websites, Amazon and others.

Interview with Jeremy Oldland, Chief Operating Officer, Hatley.

Founding

Little Blue House was founded in 1989/1990 in North Hatley in the Eastern Townships of Quebec by John Oldland, an ex-advertising man and business professor at Bishop's University, and his wife Alice, a nurse, small store owner and a very talented OCA graduate graphic artist. They sold clothing with humorous cartoon figures of farmyard animals like pigs and cows and other animals like sheepdogs, bears and moose on items like aprons, oven mitts, potholders and chef's hats. Local production was sourced. Following success at trade shows like the Toronto Gift Show they added T-shirts.   Their early success encouraged them to expand the business into other types of clothing and gift items. Their primary sales outlets were through wholesale operations gradually moving into the US. Product sourcing was initially from Canada and then internationally, primarily India. John continued his teaching and wrote up business cases about their early journey.

The early success was attributed to four main factors by John Oldland in business cases he wrote for his university classes. Firstly, the designs which were universal in appeal, graphically strong and with a sense of humour. Secondly, the product was good quality, reasonably priced and in many cases, unique. Thirdly, there was a rapid pace of innovation of new products and designs. Fourth, the use of a regular sales force calling on retailers.

Succession

In 1999/2000 John and Alice were considering selling the approximately $4.5 million revenue and 8–9 employee business, but then their three sons expressed an interest in joining and running the company. First was Chris Oldland, the oldest, responsible for sales and retail operations. He had been working in the fashion industry in New York. Nicholas (Nick) joined him as Creative Director: a talented designer and illustrator who had worked with his mother on some of the early designs. He has also authored and illustrated nine children's books in English and French from "Big Bear Hug" to "Hockey in the Wild". Chris and Nick encouraged Jeremy, the youngest, to join them. Jeremy's path had been totally different, working as a software developer with the Corel technology company and a 'tech' start – up in Ottawa. Jeremy is responsible for company operations except for marketing and design. They all moved and set up the revised operation in Montreal.

As the three sons took over, significant expansion was achieved behind the expansion of the product range. They chose the name Hatley and it became the more adult brand while Little Blue House became less promoted and more focused on children's wear. Then from 2010 onwards, prompted by some feedback from their UK-based Selfridges customer, the team started a more consistent dual branding approach with Hatley primarily centred around organic and sustainable more eco-friendly and premium fashion clothing, and Little Blue House for more irreverent design giftable items. As their website expresses it:

"The Hatley brand is best known for its hand illustrated prints and skillfully crafted premium apparel for babies, kids and women. Loaded with charming details, every Hatley piece is sure to become a cherished memory marker and future hand-me-down. Famous for its unbelievably soft, organic cotton pajamas kids adore, Hatley also tackles rainy days with a hard-wearing rainwear collection that includes colour changing prints, as well as summertime living with its beautiful and functional sunproof swimwear line."

In contrast:

"The Little Blue House brand has always been an unabashedly irreverent brand of giftable items. Made famous by its cheeky puns and unique nature-inspired prints that adorn matching family pajamas (including fur babies), women's sleepshirts, men's boxer briefs, socks, tea towels, and so many more items. A classic loungewear collection inspired by our Canadian heritage completes the range."

Operations

The source of their clothing is offshore. About 50% from family - owned businesses in India which account for the majority of the organic lines. Another 50% comes from China, especially any clothing needing zippers.

About 50% of their sales come through their wholesale operations selling to some 4,000 retailers including majors such as Hudson's Bay and Indigo in Canada; Harrods and the John Lewis Partnership in the UK; the 45-store David Jones in Australia and Nordstrom and independents in the US and Canada. Another 25% is sold via their own online activities and web sites for both Hatley and Little Blue House. Another 25% is sold through their own retail outlets. Currently there are around 33 stores in Canada, the US and the UK.

As Jeremy points out, the key is in having these channel strategies work together so that retail and online customers can be addressed and encouraged to be loyal and regular customers while continuing to build their brand reputations which itself helps the wholesale demand.

Trade shows remain key to promoting the wholesale business in the US and Canada. There are about 15 shows/year that they attend in a non-pandemic year. In Canada there are 5 – 6 shows/year they normally attend, including the Canadian Gift & Tableware Association shows. In the US, while in 2021/22 many were cancelled, they had just completed the Atlanta show. In the UK and Europe, trade show activity had been on the decline even pre-Covid so none are being attended. They have Trade Sales Representatives covering this segment of the business. As Jeremy comments:

"These shows are not just selling and marketing opportunities, they are customer service."

As far as the growing retail and online business was concerned, one of the errors and learning that Jeremy admits to is underinvesting in marketing communication and promotion. The two brands used to spend about 9% in advertising/sales (A/S) activity, around $500k/year.

"I was being mean! One year I was looking at our web and our online advertising and realized I was being small minded. We were getting great returns."

Jeremy has now increased this spending to around $1 million, about 12% A/S, more in line with what US SME organizations spend. With more legislative restrictions in data collection in social media, Hatley are now focusing on using information from their retail and online customers to understand, and meet customer needs and market to them.

Hatley competitors are many: from general clothing competitors to specialist gift and/or specialist and children's clothing specialists like 'Lazy One' from Utah; 'Tea Collection' in San Francisco and others.

Success Factors

Some 20 years on from when the brothers took over, why has this family business worked so well? Jeremy's view is five key reasons.

First, mutual respect between the brothers, and continuous communication which means they can move fast when they agree on a course of action:

"It is management by triumvirate. None of us share responsibilities. Nick is a pure designer with 12 designers and illustrators who work for him.

Money goes in one end and designs come out the other end! Chris is a 'road warrior'! He's never at home office and is always visiting our locations and clients. I am here, I'm a computer guy and now actually running our business, especially customer service. So, we don't actually overlap."

The second reason he cites is:

"We let each other make mistakes. And boy have we made some big ones."

Jeremy talks about store openings which didn't work out despite large investment. Designs that didn't sell. Business system problems like major trademark/URL issues in China. The key is:

"… to own the mistake, then roll with them and learn. Suck it up and get on with the next day!"

The three sons primarily focus on future opportunities in achieving a consistent 10% yearly growth. Hatley has developed a very positive working culture at all levels. They have a very talented, motivated senior management group that has been with the company for a long time, and are largely left to run day-to-day operations. It comprises two senior executives, one running all the day to day business and a Chief Designer. In addition to salary, they get a small profit share. They have senior managers as heads of Sales, Marketing, Finance, Retail, Operations, Customer Service and a Warehouse manager. In addition, they have senior managers running their UK and India operations. These managers are each running their sections of the business and are an integrated part of the organization's decision making. As Jeremy tells them:

"Run the business as if you own the business."

The third reason is both the quality of their products and the designs and that they are one of only a few fashion clothing companies with a strong gift business.

"With illustrators on staff we have greater flexibility as we tailor our store assortments to local needs."

The fourth reason is increased attention to their selling and marketing communications mix. Applying and integrating learning and data from across their wholesale, retail and online activity has been invaluable.

Knowledge garnered from their wholesaler customer demand feeds their retail location and marketing communications decisions. Both feed their online marketing, and that channel 's data feeds back to the other two. A virtuous circle of customer knowledge and service is formed.

The fifth reason is the quality of their staff at all levels. They have the usual turnover but many staff return due to the positive culture. This gives them depth of experience throughout its operations.

Recent Challenges

Like all SMEs they have had their challenges. Most recently, of course, the pandemic which Jeremy describes as:

"Harrowing, gut wrenching! Within a very short period all our retail stores shut. Then even the warehouse except for essential services. We went from 330 employees to about 40 in about 10 days (then it took about 9 weeks to build it back up to about 180 people!). It was a roller coaster ride."

It forced them to review operations and expenses. As a result:

"We closed 9 non-performing stores, but subsequently opened another 9 in different and better locations: for instance, in the U.K., we shut Chiswick and opened Richmond based on increasing understanding of their customers."

Similar moves were made in the US.

Further impacts were felt with wholesale clients, who cut back orders but didn't totally discontinue, and who understood supply chain problems so were more relaxed about delivery timetables. Impacts also were seen in product – type demand. For example, as Jeremy said:

"With everyone at home we sold a lot of pajamas"

During that initial period of the pandemic in 2020, in early March and before their year-end at the end of April, they made major cost cutting decisions, but as he says:

"We had the blessing of our bank, the blessing of our accountant, of our customers and the blessing of our government."

Jeremy credits the early actions of the Canadian government, and especially the subsidies as most effective and helpful. It helped them and others "*make it through.*"

Most importantly it enabled them to hire back valued employees and maintain the depth of experience.

Their early investment in online marketing helped enormously as they were able to expand the use of this channel. The knowledge of their customer base from the several channels described earlier has been one of the key factors in their ongoing success.

All of these changes were handled successfully:

"*If you can't pivot, forget about it.*"

The Future

As Jeremy and the family ponder the future, they see several challenges but continued opportunities.

Challenges include:

Cost Management. Along with all businesses they are confronting increasing inflation. Hatley costs are approaching 15% increases. These are a combination of product production and delivery costs but also labour costs. As such management of their costs and the impact on their pricing will be a major issue.

Personnel shortages. They are experiencing significant human resources shortages in a number of areas of their operations. HR is a very challenging issue these days: retaining talented employees and attracting new ones. Like many they are expanding the size and scope of their management in India as a result.

Opportunities include:

Expansion of the retail business in promising areas particularly in the US but also, for example, Vancouver.

Continuation of their substantial growth in online sales.

Continued improvement of the product to stay relevant.

Continued strength of the gift and leisure clothing market they compete in: formal clothing suppliers have not been so fortunate recently.

Acquisition: they are in the process of launching a third brand range based on a recent acquisition of an exciting gift-oriented organization that offers children's books/pajama packages.

Overall, as Jeremy sees it, with their talented management team, supplier relations and integrated distribution and marketing approach, they will continue their 10% yearly growth and this SME will continue as one of Canada's success stories:

"When it comes down to it, the product line has to constantly improve, adjust and stay relevant. There is every reason to believe we have been doing that and will continue to do so."

Interviews: Jeremy: January 17th, 21st and 26th 2022.

John: February 7th 2022.

6

SME MARKETING CHALLENGE #6: BUILDING YOUR INTERNATIONAL BUSINESS

"When you start something today, you usually have to start it all over the world at the same time to be successful."

Bernard Arnault, 1949 – date. French, Chairman and CEO LVMH.

Aided by new capabilities in technology, new products and services can seek markets outside of local or domestic markets. Improvements in logistics for shipping and delivery have meant that goods as well as services can spread their wings globally. Furthermore, the rise of e-commerce platforms like Alibaba, Amazon, eBay, Flipkart, JD, Newegg, Otto, Rakuten and Walmart mean that international retail opportunities have been growing rapidly driven by huge global growth in buying on-line which is now estimated to be over 20% of all global retail sales. Whatever the short-term impacts of some national protectionism, an international strategy for SMEs must be considered to achieve sustainable growth.

While Canada's major export market for **goods** remains the US, the following are also significant markets for Canadian goods, accounting for over #1 billion sales in 2020: China, UK, Japan, Mexico, Germany, Netherlands, South Korea, France, Italy, India, Belgium, Norway, Brazil, Australia, Hong Kong, Switzerland, Indonesia, South-East Asia, UAE, Saudi Arabia and Spain. International competition comes from more than these markets as evidenced from where we import goods: in addition to the export list in 2020 we imported over $1 billion from the following countries so these too represent opportunities: Vietnam, Peru, Ireland, Sweden, Poland, Austria, South Africa, Taiwan, Chile, Bangladesh, Cambodia and Denmark. The major markets for export revenue for **services** are the US (54% of Canada's total services export revenue), UK (6%), China (3%), France (3%), and Switzerland (2%). Our import market competitors for services are primarily the US, UK, Hong Kong, Mexico and France.

So how to decide whether to compete internationally and where to go compete?

The first step lies in the product/service the SME has developed. Where would it have an opportunity? Base your answer on some quick on-line research and your connections and contacts (see *"SME Marketing Challenge #1"* chapter). If the initial thought is that there is opportunity internationally then the product/service development process should take account of competitive offerings in two or three of those international target markets. Additionally, the SME should start the brand and URL registration process for those markets, (" *SME Marketing Challenge #2"* chapter).

As the export/import data shows, and driven by geographic and linguistic proximity and a favorable exchange rate, the US is nearly always the first thought. In many cases this is the right thought, but there are issues to consider why this should not be the only country or even the first.

1. By launching only in the US or as the first country, the SME is alerting global competitors about the product/service and its benefits and brand and thereby potentially giving up any further international sales. It may allow the development of powerful competition that will enter the home market, and possibly the US, in the future.

2. While the US is large and attractive, it is a hypercompetitive market. As one SME with which I was involved tells it, in Canada when selling their goods to retailers there would be around 3 – 5 competitors in supplier meetings. When they moved into the US there were days of meetings where 300-500 would present their brands!! It was much more difficult to gain attention beyond pricing as to the brand's distinct proposition. Large Canadian companies like Canadian Tire have found this hypercompetitive market overwhelming and Tim Hortons found extreme difficulty, though a few like Lululemon have found success.

3. There is often an assumption that socially and culturally Americans and Canadians are the same. 'Target' stores in their entry to Canada made that mistake. In an international cultural study (Hofstede) the following major cultural contrasts were found: on a 100-point scale:

   - Individualism versus Collectivism orientation: US, at a score of 91 was much more individualistic than Canada at a score of 80.

   - Masculinity values versus Femininity values: US at a score of 62 had more masculine values than Canada at 52.

   - Long term orientation versus short term: US was very short term oriented at a score of 26 while Canada was much less at a score of 36.

   - Products/services that fit Canadian desires are not necessarily the same as the US. Additionally, Canada's rate of adoption of new technologies and products/services is slower than the US so our acceptance of new ideas may already lag developments in the US.

4. Entry to other than US markets that are less hyper competitive but still attractive in potential can give the SME experience in managing international expansion. With success in these markets, they can also build up resources for a better funded US entry.

I am not attempting to dissuade SMEs from US entry, merely alerting them to other alternatives and to prepare them for a tough market, albeit sizable and attractive.

In considering an international market for entry, consideration should be given to preparation in budget and timing:

• Market research suggested in earlier chapters in this book must be extended to gaining a view on the target market's economy, exchange rates and their customer culture and behaviors. While no economic or exchange rate forecasts are totally accurate, they can help the SME develop appropriate plans and contingencies, especially with regard to exchange rate impacts.

• The more unique or superior the brand proposition, a quicker entry to key markets should be considered and a sufficiently large market entry budget raised. The second worst failure of SMEs after failing to enter promising international markets, is to enter but without sufficient funds to sustain the entry. This merely invites competition to learn and overtake the early entry. Sufficient marketing funds should be identified and raised before actual entry.

• Learning from any market, but particularly international markets, in the early days is critical. Some markets take longer to respond to new brand propositions, some are quicker. There must be continuous feedback on the acceptance and effectiveness of the different elements of the brand proposition and adjustments made. In one instance in Japan where I was involved, the primary retailer that had been engaged was found to be purposely slowing the sales to protect other brands. We had to change distribution strategy that initially resulted in lower sales coverage, but within six months was exceeding in both coverage and sales.

- Those SMEs providing on-line services (like software) to multiple markets need to follow the same advice as above but instead of focusing on geographic markets, should focus on trends in the industry sectors and customers they serve. This will help them understand trends and competitors thereby providing information for service improvement and expansion. Getting to know how your customer is using (or not fully using) your service is critical to ensuring the customer is getting the best value from it and potentially helps identify new opportunities.

- The point is that once you are serving a customer, understand how it helps them and their business so that you can constantly improve the value of your relationship with them.

While international expansion is not for all SMEs it should be a realistic option for many. To quote a famous phrase in strategy for our tools:

SME Marketing Challenge Tool #6: "Think Global but Act Local"

- In your business planning consider whether your target groups are purely local or international (especially technology – based products/services).

- Given the existence of global media to reach these target groups and global competition, plan your strategy to enable sale to global customers if it represents a significant opportunity.

- Plan your resources appropriately: the extent and timing of your global activity will be impacted by available resources. Be warned, if you have a breakthrough product or service, launch in only a local market may tip competition into moving first into other markets.

- As you view the Marketing Mix 10, don't keep going with data from your local market, source data from other important local markets. You may need adjustments to different elements of the marketing mix to better meet local needs: language, features emphasized, pricing, delivery logistics etc.

- Protect your core customer base, whether global or local, so manage expansion carefully.

- Learn from US and international companies for insight not only into international markets but also domestically – as did Sleep Country.

Global expansion of your business is not just for expansionary reasons but for protection. By not taking the product/service abroad, organizations may soon find international competitors learning and entering the home market with a directly competitive or next generation product/service.

Be careful where you expand and how: international sales team from home office, sales agent, subsidiary etc. Do it with research that gives you understanding of the culture and environment, the competition and set realistic expectations. While international business is often much larger than domestic business, it is more complex and can take a longer time. Be sure your base business, if it is domestic, is in good shape. Canada needs more SMEs competing globally, don't rule it out!

SME Story 6.1. Umbra

Umbra is a successful medium sized enterprise designing and selling contemporary home décor products internationally. Winner of numerous design awards and inducted into the Canada's Marketing Hall of Legends as Visionaries.

Founded in Toronto in 1979, Umbra is currently just under $200 million revenue with 483 personnel. It sells some 600 – 700 core Umbra branded items and in total of more than 2,000 contemporary design home products. They operate via the head office in Toronto and satellite offices in Brazil, China, the Netherlands and the US to over 25,000 retailers in 120 countries as well as direct sales from its web site and through Amazon.

Interview with Les Mandelbaum, President, co-founder/owner.

Founding

Founded in 1979 by childhood friends Les Mandelbaum (then a bass player in a band) and Paul Rowan (another musician but chiefly a designer), Umbra is now a global creator and seller of contemporary design home décor products (*"Original. Modern. Casual."*). It sells through general retailers, direct order from its web site and Amazon, and stores in 120 countries.

Les and Paul started a part time business in 1979 selling window shades with attractive, contemporary graphics under the brand Umbra Shades.

"Casual, cool looking, cash and carry that you could install yourself."

Sensing bigger opportunities, and with Les coming from an entrepreneurial family, and Paul a talented, trained graphic designer, they decided to expand operations and changed the name to just Umbra (which itself is Latin for a fully shaded region of a shadow). As Les indicates, taking the challenge:

"To provide cool products for the home that were affordable and with more contemporary designs."

Their target group was the boomer generation family-formers who wanted a design break from that of their parents.

They sourced funds from bank credit and by 1982 were designing and sourcing contemporary design and practical home products like trash cans, picture frames and clocks. Then, following consumer trends and business opportunities from a growing type of specialty chain retailers in the US like Bed, Bath & Beyond, Crate & Barrel, and Pottery Barn, they added items like place mats, drapery rods, kitchen storage and other items growing from 50 to 100 contemporary design products.

"We had some big hits like trash cans, cool vinyl place mats, picture frames, clocks, drapery rods for cash and carry. We had the first good looking trash can....and we still do. We made trash cans respectable."

Growth

In the high interest rate period of 1985, their bank which had provided lining credit reduced the amount, so Umbra went through a consolidation period tightening costs. At that time Canadian banks would not fund US receivables, so they switched to a US bank that would, which helped prepare them for the next decades of major growth. By the early 1990s they were fully self-funding.

Their primary sales and marketing activity was through trade shows. The big US shows like the New York Gift Show and the International Home + Housewares Show in Chicago also attracted many overseas buyers. From this start Umbra started to gain wholesale and retail customers internationally, especially in Europe, Japan and gradually in South East Asia. Building on this success, they began to establish their own operations in the Netherlands, in Amsterdam, which became their European and Middle East headquarters. They also set up an Umbra–owned warehouse in Buffalo to handle US distribution, offices in Sao Paulo, Brazil for Central and South America, Japan through a partner/distributor, and then China.

While 10% of their product lines such as trash cans are made domestically, remaining products are sourced offshore. China is their manufacturing source for about 90% of their products so they set up in Hong Kong and Shenzhen to handle the relations with local manufacturing suppliers.

They expanded their trade show attendance to major global shows like Ambiente in Frankfurt and expanded their sales team and online promotion, especially through Amazon. In Toronto in 2007 they opened their Retail Design Award winning store. As Les describes it:

"A great branding and real estate investment!"

By 2020/2021 their business was truly global: about 40% of sales in the US, 25% in Europe, 15% in Canada, 10 - 12% in Latin America and the rest internationally.

Product design was key to their success. They supplemented the work of their 10 internal designers headed by Matt Carr, with other respected external names like Karim Rashid, Hlynur Atlason and Harry Allen. In 1996 Rashid and Umbra created the famous GARBO trash can (named after the actress Greta Garbo) which sold over two million units in just two years, and then a miniature version (GARBINO) that sells today. The original is now in the permanent collection of the Museum of Modern Art (MoMa) in New York. Rashid also designed the OH Chair for Umbra (the original is also at MoMa). Their beautifully designed home products range through bathrooms (soap pumps, toothbrush holders etc.), kitchens (dish racks etc.), dining rooms (napkin holders etc.), bedrooms (jewelry tree, jewelry box, make-up mirrors etc.) and all home areas (storage boxes etc.). They sell some 2,000 items including private label supply and 600+ core Umbra branded products.

Umbra's product development strategy discussed at their twice monthly design meetings is to create products where about one third are *"market driven"*: a better design of existing products like a paper towel holder and mirrors. About one third are *"derivations"*: additional versions of existing products like picture frames. About one third are *"blue sky/ unexpected/outlier"* items like their "Strumba Kalimba", a classical musical thumb piano based on a Zimbabwean instrument.

In discussing their product success rate, Les describes their experience:

"We're making fantastic products. In terms of acceptance, we used to have a third, a third, a third. A third of the products were complete duds: we thought they were a great idea but who knows what the customer and consumer really wants to buy. A third were good, made good money and were well accepted. A third could go either way: could be good or bad. Now we are a little smarter about it and applying the formula we use, now two-thirds of our products are successful."

While Paul retired at the end of 2016, Umbra had already built a strong management team working with Les. Matt Carr, their Chief Designer, has been with them 21 years; Joseph Adamo, Executive VP Operations and Chief Financial Officer, 10 years; Tariq Jamal, Chief Information Officer, 11 years; Henry Huang, head of product development and manufacturing in China; Mark Benson, VP Sales based in Chicago. Joining them more recently have been Sonja Smith, Director Human Resources, and Yael Grimman, VP Global Marketing, and ex-Dyson Europe manager, another strong entrepreneurial company. This stability helped them through the impact of three big issues in early 2020: the pandemic, Brexit in the UK and the current supply chain challenges.

The Post-Pandemic Business.

When the pandemic hit in early 2020, the shut downs occurred in nearly all their markets. They furloughed 10% of their staff, laid some off (their trade show representatives), lowered their manufacturing orders, closed the Toronto store and stepped up their online promotion. Their business through Amazon and other online channels went from around 20% of total sales to 50%. Through early 2020 there was virtually no business.

"It was hell! We had no business for about a month, then some came back online: the channels shifted."

Canadian and Ontario Government subsidy programs eventually helped lower the impact. By the summer business was recovering and the full year 2020 was not too bad. However, the pandemic effects along with global political developments created a number of other business challenges for 2021 and 2022. As Les commented:

"The earthquake was the pandemic, the tsunami/the flood that did most of the damage was what came afterwards."

- Both manufacturing and supply chain costs are increasing and timing of the supply and quantities are big issues.

- Additionally, changes in China and Hong Kong government policies are creating further sourcing challenges. While not major at this point in time, Umbra is investigating supply from Vietnam, Bangladesh and other sources, though right now have not relocated due to Covid restrictions.

- In the UK, Brexit was devastating for retail orders due to new import regulations and duties and growing labour shortages impacting the supply chain. Costs rose enormously. Germany took over from the UK as Umbra's biggest market. For the rest of Europe and Asia (Japan, Australia, New Zealand, Singapore) demand for home goods continues strong and in Europe prices increases have been more accepted.

- While in the US the at-home effects of the pandemic improved demand for home goods, costs of product production and supply increased. The US government imposed an additional 20% duties on China–sourced goods. Umbra found it difficult to take the needed 10% price increases quickly enough. Home goods margins are not high in normal times, so Umbra has found its margins squeezed.

"Price negotiations are tough right now. It's easier to do these in person, tougher online. Bad news is better communicated in person."

- In all markets Umbra is experiencing labour shortages and salary/ wage increases at all levels having impacts on work processes, logistics, administration and other costs to this day.

E-commerce now accounts for nearly half their business: the pandemic accelerated what was already happening. It meant that instead of just shipping from Toronto and Buffalo in the US, they had to set up other centres.

"I would say, logistics has become as important as the product now."

In the last year (2021), while their revenues have remained at around $200 million, margins are being severely squeezed and based on this Umbra is investigating changes in all aspects of its business. Itself a clue to its success in the past and a lesson for all SMEs for the future.

Lessons from Umbra

- Understand the core of your business and keep innovating. In Umbra's case this is unique and original designs, of great quality at good prices for items for the home. This difference is at the heart of Umbra's success in a low margin industry where there are limited available marketing communication funds. Umbra's primary marketing advantage is the distinctiveness of its products and the positive reputation for the brand that they have built.

As Les says:

"Our marketing is our product. And we help and rely on good consumer and customer experience to get the word out"

- Investigate and learn where opportunities lie. In Umbra's case, this meant following up on contacts at US trade shows wherever they were globally and then building an infrastructure to serve them.

- Build a management team and culture that respect each other and the customers. Give family members a chance to engage but don't force it. Les has two sons who have some involvement but have their own interests, so he will see where life takes them. Right now, at 70 years young, Les says:

"I have no immediate plans to retire. I don't think retirement would be healthy for me."

- Where at all possible, be ethically and ecologically "sound".

- As an owner *"don't believe your own press"!*

- Have fun!

Interview: January 25th 2022.

7

SME MARKETING CHALLENGE #7: SCALING UP – EXECUTIVE MARKETING MANAGEMENT.

"A big business starts small"

Sir Richard Branson; 1950 – date; British, founder and owner Virgin Group

One of Canada's challenges in developing a thriving SME sector is that after initial success, Canadian SMEs do not successfully 'scale up" to further success as extensively as other countries. Statistics Canada and BDC research indicates that some 87% of Canadian businesses remain as a small size enterprise and only 2% move from medium size to large (500+ employees). The changes that do occur happen during the first 5 years of the organization. The reasons for success are:

- The enterprises are more productive than competitors.

- They invest more in fixed assets and staff.

- They market across Canada and in some cases internationally.

The reasons for the poor scale-up record are many:

- Many sell their enterprise shortly after a successful 'start-up'. They see an opportunity to maximize the personal value of their efforts at an early stage. US SMEs, in contrast, want to build commercial empires while many Canadians are happy to gather early returns and exit.

- Some fail to sustain their initial success due to new or more aggressive competition domestically or internationally.

- Some fail because they do not have the resources or the inclination to continue to develop their product/service or spend sufficiently on marketing to promote it.

- But the evidence is that most fail because they have not developed sufficiently deep management skill as the enterprise gets larger and more complex.

It is this latter area that we will focus on in this chapter. There is a tendency amongst some entrepreneurs to continue to make all key decisions themselves. As an enterprise gets larger and more complex, this approach can become dysfunctional and retard adaption and agility. Successful SMEs continue the drive, energy and insight of its founders but add the capabilities of professional managers and staff. This is true in all areas but particularly in marketing. As we noted in an earlier chapter (*SME Marketing Challenge #1*), Canadian SMEs underspend on marketing activity so leadership in this area is particularly important.

During the start-up phases of SME development, it is quite usual and appropriate to have the founders making all important decisions. In family enterprises this can be quite widespread crossing generations. After initial success and as the SMEs grow, the scope and frequency of important decision-making increases exponentially. Unless the principals of the enterprise can rely on experienced and capable decisions and implementation from others, the danger of slow or over narrow decision-making by the principal(s) can harm the enterprise. Bringing on appropriate and experienced executives to aid in the SME decision making regarding new challenges can aid in the adjustment of enterprise strategy to these challenges. Diversity of experienced and well–considered input at these times is at the heart of needed innovation in areas like product/service development, production, financing, and importantly, sales and marketing. In one organization that I was involved with previously, the founder of the company was not adapting his approach to changes with customers in his key export market, Japan. On my advice he brought in experienced professional management as President and chose the role of Chairman for himself. He essentially became an 'ambassador' for the company with customers and an advisor and counsel to the President. The company trebled sales and profitability within 2 years! The lessons to achieve successful 'scale-up' are many and do vary enterprise by enterprise, but in addition to those marketing issues covered in the previous chapters, they include:

- Recognition that, within affordability constraints, the key assets of an enterprise are not only its intellectual property and brand, but the talent of the executives, managers and staff that work for it.

- Contributing to this value are the additions of executives and managers who not only have the capability but also relevant experience and can bring that experience into the enterprise to help in scale-up decisions.

- Having hired the right people, the challenge to the SME founder is to listen to those executives and build an effective decision-making team. Hiring talent but not listening to it does not build positive returns. One very experienced and successful marketing executive friend of mine was hired by a start-up Cannabis enterprise in Toronto. In eighteen months, the founder did not accept one recommendation from him despite strong rationale. My friend quit and the enterprise is now struggling. In contrast, in another case where I was consulting with a Canadian multinational B2B enterprise with manufacturing plants in Pickering, Ontario, the US, Germany and China, I commented to the founder how good his executives were (and well paid!). His response was that he loved getting and keeping the best people to help make him even more money. How smart is that attitude!

- Smart professionals working for a scaling-up enterprise not only need to be listened to but rewarded for their success. Remuneration strategies should recognize the risk and reward issues that any SME faces but build enterprise commitment to share the responsibilities for the risks and to reap the rewards.

- A US Association of Chartered Certified Accountants (ACCA) 2018 research and report *"Scale Up Success – What do SMEs need to supercharge* their *growth"* emphasizes the importance of building a coherent growth strategy which includes not only technological and financial considerations but:

  o Clear purpose and vision.

  o A planned organization structure involving experienced senior executives.

  o An outlook which emphasizes the marketing issues of a full customer understanding (" Customer 360"), a global perspective and access to the advice of veterans in the business or the sector ("Venture Veterans").

  o Organization behaviors that emphasize the importance of networking with customers and other organizations ("Meeters and Greeters") and finding the early adopters of the product/ service and getting them to act as influencers.

The report is well worth accessing: www.accaglobal.com.

Canada needs SMEs of all shapes and sizes, from start-ups to successful home-grown major successes like Shopify. To get there, a balance of all management skills, resources and risk taking and courage is required. In many cases, this means bringing in experienced and motivated talent at all levels, including senior management. If you bring them in, listen to them.

Think of three characteristics of who might make great additions to your enterprise. Obviously, you want someone who has great talent and can add specific or general experience where you need it – maybe in marketing, maybe in sales etc. Also, be sure they have the personality and attitude that fits with the culture and size of your SME. Many highly talented executives whose careers have only been in large organizations have difficulty transitioning to smaller, less resourced organizations. If you know the individuals or they are family, this often helps but it can cause other problems.

SME Marketing Challenge Tool #7: Scaling – Up: Talent, Experience and Attitude

As you go through the selection process, keep these characteristics in mind:

- Be clear about what skills you need: talent, training and experience. Especially look for skills and experiences you don't have and/or are needed in areas where your markets are developing.

- Be sure you are comfortable with the salary and expense budget necessary to attract and retain them.

- Be clear about your willingness to listen to their talent and experience and act on it. Be prepared to consider what may initially seem radical recommendations.

- Look for the attitude that will enable them to thrive in a smaller organization with less resources than they may have been used to.

- Look at their proven ability to work closely with clients and also motivate staff.

- Make sure you reference check widely to ensure 'fit' with you and your goals.

- Consider using a professional search firm, preferably one that you feel knows you and your ambitions.

SME Story 7.1. Mother Raw

A growing, Toronto-based small size company developing, manufacturing, marketing and selling organic and plant-based dressings & marinades, condiments and dips in Canada and the US.

Originally founded as RawFoodz in 2010 in Toronto by Michelle Kopman who started by selling her plant-based organic dressings at farmer's markets and local stores. In 2016, after an investment from Whitecap Venture Partners and a few individual investors, growth of RawFoodz lagged expectations. In late 2017, Kristi Knowles was brought in as a consultant to assess the situation. In early 2018, shortly after the sad early death of Michelle, Kristi was appointed CEO to lead the vision and activate her recommendations, including a full rebranding effort. In January 2019, the company unveiled Mother RawTM. to North America, remaining faithful to Michelle's core proposition but with new branding, formulations, products and innovations in marketing and operations. Since then, and through the pandemic, with its 20 staff, it has gained positive attention, distribution and sales from both Canada and the US.

Interview with Kristi Knowles, CEO Mother Raw.

RawFoodz

The original founding of the company as RawFoodz by Michelle Kopman goes back to 2010. She had built a successful but limited operation selling plant based, organic, minimally processed, refrigerated salad dressings and a few other similar products. In 2016, Whitecap Venture Partners along with two senior executives from the food industry, set up Reunion Foods Inc. which invested in RawFoodz to accelerate its growth.

In the early RawFoodz website Michelle described their business as follows:

"We manufacture raw, vegan, organic, nut-free, gluten-free, kosher, superfood infused dressings, dips & spreads. All traditional style, yet made with nature's most wholesome, health promoting, immune boosting, weight loss promoting ingredients."

Whitecap brought in Kristi Knowles to work as a consultant with Michelle and the executive team on a total rebranding strategy. Kristi had mostly completed the strategic plan when sadly Michelle, aged only 45 years old, died in February 2018.

Michelle had two children, too young at the time to join the business, though her oldest, her daughter Laurel, 19 at the time, was involved by Kristi in the rebranding effort. As a summer student, she was able to be at the table as decisions were made about the future of the company. On Michelle's death, Whitecap offered the CEO role to Kristi.

Kristi Knowles, the consultant then CEO brought in by Whitecap, is one of Canada's most experienced and respected executives. With a marketing and sales career spanning some 30 years in food and beverage at Unilever, Campbell's and Molson Coors and management and Board volunteer work in health and food industries, Kristi was a perfect choice to create the vision for the brand and the company.

The consulting work was done with Kristi's usual thoroughness, consumer research and with Michelle's input. The first task was to make the products accessible to more people. The basic proposition was spot on. However, a decision was made to broaden the proposition for a wider audience, including moving away from vegan communication and towards plant-based messaging. Additionally, recipes were overhauled given that great taste and product performance trumped other considerations. The branding and design were the next challenges to tackle. Kristi comments:

"RawFoodz is not a strong brand name: it's a descriptor, didn't have wide appeal and was limiting. Also, the branding and design elements didn't reflect the premium or organic nature of the product. So, all things consumer facing had to evolve quickly while building the team."

A plan was developed for a go-to-market strategy with taste improvements and rebranding at the top of the agenda. At the time the organization had grown from producing a handful of self-manufactured products to around 13 SKUs. All had no nuts, gluten, soy, canola, preservatives or fillers. Sold through some 30 stores in Canada, their gross sales volume was well under $500,000/year.

After Kristi took the CEO position, her first task was, as she puts it:

"When the founder of the company dies, it's as if all the lights go out. My job was to turn the lights back on, and do it in an open, transparent way to protect the business's reputation."

Mother Raw launch

From March 2018 to the launch of Mother Raw in January 2019 Kristi and the team worked tirelessly. Michelle had been the product developer and holistic nutritionist, so with Whitecap's backing Kristi hired a head of product development and a contract holistic nutritionist. Their original head of product development came from France where additive use was minimal so her experience was very relevant. Initially they focused on the top selling dressings while after they worked on new products:

"We created our own tasting panel with 25 people and were cycling through, recipe after recipe after recipe: too many tastings to count!"

As they started on the rebranding process, Kristi brought in the Zulu Alpha Kilo advertising agency. The new branding merged elements of the rawness of Mother Earth, organic design elements and a sense of playfulness.

"The team at Mother Raw takes our products and what we do very seriously so that our consumers can really enjoy them. We created a mission that is simple yet powerful: 'to encourage people to eat more plants. Why? Because it just makes good sense."

The work with the agency culminated with the new brand name, Mother Raw, new design and the brand motto 'Put Good on Good'.

As the business scaled up, they grew their full-time production staff, now about 10 people, and fine-tuned the manufacturing process. It is now a highly efficient and very collaborative process that allows the team great autonomy in their work. They also have an employee solely responsible for product safety given the business's commitment to health and safety.

"We are extremely proud of our health and safety record and confidently maintain all certifications including: non-GMO, organic, vegan and kosher."

Through the pandemic they kept operating, gained new distribution and added new SKUs of salad dressing, dips and Quesos. Taste was a key criterion along with the plant-based proposition.

As Kristi says:

"What we did was an important evolution of the food, and revolution of the branding but all grounded on the same vision as the founder."

They stepped up online marketing communications, setting up separate Canadian (English and French) and US web sites to allow for direct-to-consumer shipments.

Gaining new distribution was tough, especially during the peak of the 2020/2021 Covid period, but Kristi's sales team and her own time in sales management with Unilever made them resilient and capable of pivoting to meet new challenges.

"With scrappy, optimistic, resilient, likeable and very experienced sales leads, we've broken through barriers that many companies of our size have struggled with."

Produce buyers in retailers were their key prospects. They tended to be very regional in their orientation, so the Mother Raw distribution strategy took that focus. Their targeted distributors and retailers were based on segmentation research indicating what consumer profiles would be most attracted by the Mother Raw brand proposition.

Sustained Growth

The rebranding, new product development and distribution strategies were successful through 2019 to date. The pandemic certainly had an initial effect but the combination of the great planning, execution and the quality of the products combined with a growth in home-prepared meals saw their success continue. Distribution grew to almost 5,000 stores including specialty and chain stores in the US like Meijer in the Midwest (250+ stores), Pavilions in southern California, Sprouts Farmers Market (300 + stores), and Whole Foods. In Canada, other than Quebec, they are in Fortinos, Longo's, Metro, Save-On-Foods,

Sobeys and Walmart. In terms of product range, they now have 25 SKUs and more to come. The refrigerated dip category alone is already an estimated $1.1 billion market in North America.

In late 2020, about $8.1 million further funding was raised by Whitecap and new investors Forage Capital and the Export Development Corporation. The growth continues, driven by a senior team that includes Kristi, Ian Fraser Head of Operations, and Brent Lunn, Head of Sales. They added to their sales staff with an executive who focuses on Canada and South-Western US sales. Brent is now focused on new brokers and new retailers. The company also gains from Kristi's involvement with a group of 50 Canadian food industry founders and Plant Based Foods Canada, where there is not only advice and experience, but potential opportunities for synergistic cooperation.

As they look to 2022 and beyond, everyone, investors and staff, are what Kristi calls:

"Impatiently patient"

Optimism driven by the growth in demand for organic, plant-based and 'clean' foods and Mother Raw's growing expertise and reputation.

Lessons

Kristi's learning and tips for others includes:

- In the plant-based and organic food industry great taste matters, especially for repeat purchase. Create an objective taste panel and get honest feedback. Pay for professional sensory research if affordable.

- You can precisely segment your messaging in this digital environment, so make sure your brand proposition is broad enough to capture the widest legitimate audience:

"Speak plant-based and you can attract vegan. Communicate allergen friendly and communicate specific allergens to those that care about them."

- Continually go back to your brand proposition and test that your actions remain authentic:

"Stay true to your roots."

But, don't be afraid of evolving your brand:

"Realize as early as you can when things need changing or optimizing, and get on with it."

- Invest in your culture and team. The right team makes all the difference.

- Make sure your investors are the right partners for you.

"You generally don't just want the money, but also the support, expertise and network."

- Build your own network by giving more than you are receiving and: *"You will be surprised how valuable it becomes."*

Interview: Kristi Knowles February 7th 2022.

SME Story 7.2. Pet Valu Holdings Ltd.

A small, then medium sized, and now large public company, Pet Valu is Canada's largest specialty pet store network.

Founded in 1976, Pet Valu has grown to 700 x 3,000–5,500 square foot retail stores: corporate (about 200 stores) and franchise owned (about 500 stores), and online delivery. The 1,800+ staff work under the company banners Pet Valu, Bosley's, Total Pet, Paulmac's Pets, Tisol Pet and recently, Chico in Quebec. Pet Valu offers some 7,000 products including national pet brands and has extensive and well-regarded proprietary brands such as Performatrin, Lovibles and Barker's in consumables, and Bailey and Bella, Jump, Essentials and Fresh 4 Life in hardlines and accessories. With total annual revenues of around $776 million, its rapid growth is being aided by about a 10% growth in the overall pet product marketplace of around $11 billion annually.

Interview with Tanbir Grover, Chief Digital & Marketing Officer.

Tanbir has been with Pet Valu for almost 2 years, following a senior and highly successful marketing career with Sears Canada, Hudson's Bay and Lowe's Canada. He joins an executive management team of ten headed by the President/CEO Richard Maltsbarger that includes James Grady, Chief Financial Officer, Christine Martin-Bevilacqua, Chief Administration Officer and Kendalee Mackay, Chief Merchants Officer.

Originally a pet store in north Toronto, Pet Valu was founded in 1976 by Geoffrey Holt. With the backing of Goodwood Inc. fund management, Geoffrey Holt and the family built a highly successful medium sized business in Ontario, headquartered in Markham. Their first franchise store opened in 1987 and went on to acquire other franchises across Canada such that they are now about 65% franchise stores. These now include notable and well established regional organizations that have retained their retail brand identification like Bosley's in B.C. acquired in 2010 (some 23 stores growing to 80 presently); Paulmac's Pet Food in Ontario (18 stores); Total Pet in B.C. (16 stores); Tisol in B.C. acquired in 2015 (9 stores); and in early 2022 Chico in Quebec (66 stores).

Funding their expansion after the initial period came from two events. In 2009, Roark Capital Group, an Atlanta based private equity firm, acquired Pet Valu for $144 million which enabled Tom McNeely, then President of Pet Retail Brands, to make many of the acquisitions described above. Then on June 24th 2021, they made an initial public offering on the Toronto Stock Exchange of almost 16 million shares. As Richard Maltsbarger, President and CEO commented in their most recent annual report:

"As we look ahead to 2022, we target another year of growth ahead of our long-term model. We are also excited to welcome Chico to the Pet Valu family, and positioning us to better serve Canada's devoted pet lovers with 700 stores across all 10 provinces."

The Market

Back in the 1980s and 1990s, there were only a few major pet food brands from corporations like General Mills, Mars, Quaker and Ralston-Purina. Available brands were few and accessories limited. As such, small pet food stores could meet demand as well as the limited selections in major grocery retailers.

The 2000s saw increases in the proportion of homes with pets (now about 38% own cats and 35% own dogs) plus those with birds, fish, reptiles and small animals). There was a significant increase in the number of brands and products offered as increasingly pets are seen as members of the family. Pet ownership accelerated further through the pandemic and is across all ages, demography and regions.

Products sold are not only a wide variety of consumables (wet, dry and fresh food and treats) and accessories for the pet (cat litter, clothing, collars/leashes, toys, bedding, furniture and travel). Pet services are also offered by specialist pet stores: washing, nail trimming, advice and health links to Vets and breeders.

Brands sold include national brands like Royal Canin, Whiskas and Iams from Mars Petcare; Dog Chow, Beneful and Friskies from Purina Pet Care; Meow Mix and Milk Bone from J.M. Smucker; Hills Pet Nutrition and Blue Buffalo. However, this is also a market where proprietary labels have a large share. This is part of the success of Pet Valu.

Purchase locations have been largely retail stores but this is changing. It has included general retailers like Canadian Tire, Costco, Loblaws, Metro, Sobeys, Safeway and Walmart and specialist retailers like Pet Valu but also PetSmart, Global Pet Foods, and Helmutt's Pet Supply. Now the increasing sector – already about 10% of total market – is online, direct delivery sales through specialist providers like Ren's Pets and Mondou who are offering omnichannel access via online and stores, as well as PetSmart and Pet Valu. There is also competition from general online organizations like Amazon. This has been, and is now more than ever, a highly competitive marketplace with strong attention paid to customer knowledge and care, product quality, distribution convenience and active marketing communication in external and in-store media.

As Tanbir says:

"It's a triangle: marketing is about quality, the selection to fit the customer's needs and brand expertise alongside a fair price for that."

Pet Valu Insights for Success

Pet Valu's journey from small retailer to franchisor to major Canadian presence has been marked by the 'magnificent seven' of insights:

- First, understanding the relationship with the pet owner in product and service needs, and the changes over time.

- Second, delivering local area convenience for shopping, service, and recently, delivery.

- Third, gaining the value of multiple locations concentrated by region to enable effective and efficient branding and communications.

- Fourth,a franchising model that keeps store owners close to customers and in the community is an important part of the service provided (and hence why franchisors are limited to 5stores/franchisee).

- Fifth, the importance of all staff at Pet Valu and franchisees: a culture of customer centricity.

- Sixth, proprietary brands represent a valuable addition to the offering for financial, customer choice and reputational reasons.

- Seventh, new sales channels online not only represented new ways of reaching customers but the omnichannel linkage adds to customer understanding and improved service.

1. Pet Owner Understanding and Relationship.

   The focus on one part of a customer's life, their life with pets, with the right research and attitude enabled Pet Valu's understanding of the relationships with the pet's health, welfare, happiness and domestic relationship. This enabled not only the right kind of extensive product offering, but the development of valued services, advice and community. The pet store itself becomes an important and trusted part of a pet owner's life thereby adding value beyond just pricing and selection.

2. Local Area Convenience.

   In addition to the point above, the store location needs to provide convenience for shopping and visits. Convenient locations for shopping and being in easy distance for delivery and collection has always been important, but now in an omnichannel world even more valuable for online order and delivery.

3. The Value of Area-Concentrated Multiple Locations.

Multiple locations in concentrated geographic areas enabled needed marketing communications and brand awareness building with greater affordability and efficiency. This gave a competitive advantage as it built quicker and better awareness, purchase intent, purchase and loyalty.

4. The Advantages of a Franchise Model.

Although management of a franchise system does present managerial challenges, the advantages are many as evidenced by the continued success of Tim Hortons amongst others. For Pet Valu it was:

- Economically it enables faster expansion of operations with less capital investment.

- Owner-managed operations are more likely to have higher engagement and commitment than corporate management. This is especially true with family managed operations.

- Most importantly, sourcing franchisees from within, or close to, a geographic community enables close customer knowledge and relationships.

Tanbir comments:

"Working in a franchise organization is more challenging but at the same time it holds me to a higher standard: are we delivering the right marketing messages, providing the right experiences that I would be proud of as an entrepreneur running a store?"

5. A Culture of Customer Centricity.

This orientation to people and the culture is reflected in the importance of the culture and training with front line staff. These are the people dealing directly with the customer and their pets and are seen as important advisors and helpers. Tanbir comments:

"We recognize the importance of the people that are behind our product and service, and the role they play in giving our expertise to our devoted pet lover. A lot of what we do, and must do, with franchisees and all staff is about education about both pets and new forms of communications and delivery. This ultimately leads to a customer experience we can be proud of"

6.   The Advantages of Proprietary Brands.

As many, like Loblaws with President's Choice, have proved, private labels are no longer just lower cost and quality versions of national brands. They have developed as full brand attractions themselves. Pet Valu has 11 private label offerings which account for about 30% share in their categories. These include food/consumable offerings like the Performatrin range (Naturals and Ultra), Barkers and Lovibles, and hardline and specialty brands like Kitty's Choice and Fresh4Life litter, Bailey & Bella, Jump and Essentials apparel, collars, leashes, bedding and furniture. All their proprietary brands are great quality and a number at parity or premium prices to national brands. The combination of national and proprietary brands has added to the variety offered and attraction of Pet Valu as well as both revenue and profit.

7.   Online and Omnichannel.

In the US, the success of Chewy, an online provider, has been huge, reaching over $8 billion revenue and 20+ million customers which has made it larger than PetSmart that purchased them in 2017. In Canada, both Ren's Pets and Mondou are moving from online supply to an omnichannel presence. Pet Valu has also been moving in this direction. Indeed, it was one of the reasons Tanbir was hired due to his deep background in digital retail. As he says:

"Marketing is being transformed: it is data driven marketing, performance marketing: it is a challenging area, and how we connect the digital experience to the total customer experience is critical. We are seeing all types of marketing converging as that is what customer experience is being measured on".

The key is that the crossover between store and online provides a great advantage versus a pure play online model as there is greater ability to provide service and understanding based on deeper knowledge of the customer. As he says:

"I think of Chewy as transactional. If they come to Canada, we stand out as we have our store network and different fulfillment options that get product quicker to the customer, and also the in-store experience of a pet – based local watering hole where you can bring your pet with you and have that shared experience".

Over time Pet Valu has been both a disrupter and an adopter of trends that have woken up the somewhat sleepy pet care industry. Much like Sleep Country and many of the other stories in this book, they have recognized the importance of deep customer knowledge and service and how it changes with the times. With pets, it is the deep relationships and therefore opportunities that pet owners, and particularly the pet lovers, have with their cats, dogs, birds, fish, and other animals…even pigs:

"I am fond of pigs. Dogs look up to us. Cats look down on us. Pigs treat us as equals."

Winston Churchill.

Pet Valu has been, and remains, a Canadian success story.

Interview: March 11th 2022.

8

SME MARKETING CHALLENGE #8: CONCLUDING THOUGHTS.

"The next generation of marketers and behavioral economists will enhance the economic, social and environmental contributions that marketing makes to the welfare of people and the planet."

Philip Kotler, 1931 – date, American, leading Marketing Professor, economist, author and consultant.

Marketing is constantly changing and evolving. The disciplines and practices have to keep up with changes in people's habits, preferences and attitudes, technology (especially AI systems), competition, regulation, the environment and recently the acceleration of certain changes caused by the pandemic.

One recent book from Kotler, Kartajaya and Setiawan see several trends impacting SME marketing, and indeed all marketing. While the principles outlined in this book are still all valid, some of the changes add important perspectives:

- Target segments will often take significant advice and counsel from their expanded community: what some have termed "the f-factor: family, friends, fans and followers". For some parts of our lives, we pay attention to specific online fans and followers and as such, they are an extension of the segments we should target. These customer extended networks are the target communities.

- Brand positioning is now even more important, but with constant public examination and news, exaggerated or false claims damage the brand even more.

- The elements in the Marketing Mix are still important but increasingly the customer needs to be more actively involved and, in many cases, co-create the products and services as well as the distribution networks and marketing communication activity.

- The authors suggest a new customer path given this new environment. The goals for the target segment are to move them through the following stages, the 'Five As': Aware; Appeal; Ask; Act; and Advocate. As such, in the early stages, focus on increasing attraction and optimizing curiosity about the brand; then find ways to increase commitment and increase the brand's affinity.

In order to succeed, SMEs not only need to keep up with changes in terms of the customer problems/opportunities, but ideally, get ahead of some. In another recent piece of research, Tom Eisemann, in his book and article "Why Start-Ups Fail", notes the failure of start-ups in their marketing thinking and planning marketing to:

- Properly define the target customer problem/opportunity; then

- Properly "test" the product/service solution by researching when, how, if and what value the customer places on the solution.

In further research, the Harvard Business Review in the "Spotlight" section in July/August 2021 ran a feature on "AI Powered Marketing" which emphasized how important it was now for SMEs to consider and maximize the value of AI in their marketing. As one of the articles expresses it:

> *"Humans are, by and large, reluctant to change. Many managers haven't yet adjusted to the frequency and level of detail at which technology can make old decisions."*

These areas of input are especially important in quickly learning customer changes in preference and level of satisfaction with service and adapting or responding to them.

Canadian entrepreneurs have a great history of innovation and business success, but marketing has been one of its lesser skills with some notable exceptions covered in the cases in this book and others.

Canadian SMEs need good financing, good talent and good luck but particularly these days, good marketing.

This last challenge is critical as with constant improvements in technology, and constant expansion of who competes for business (increasingly China, India, South East Asia from countries like Indonesia and Vietnam, some newly emergent African economies and Latin America as well as traditional sources of competition in the 'Triad' of U.S., Europe and Japan/Korea). Canadian businesses need to step up to these new challenges in order to avoid the vulnerability of being just a 'branch plant economy': especially its massively important SME sector.

BIBLIOGRAPHY

"Every time you state what you want or believe, you're the first to hear it. It is a message to both you and others about what you think is possible. Don't put a ceiling on yourself."

Oprah Winfrey, 1954 – date. American, media entrepreneur.

Association of Chartered Certified Accountants (ACCA) U.S, *"Scale Up Success – What do SMEs need to supercharge their growth."* Report 2018.

Bloomberg Businessweek magazine:

- July 26th, 2021, page 11, 13 "When Product Placement is the Real Star".

- January 11th, 2021, page 17 *"Bezos Bets on Podcasts"*.

Crane, Frederick G. *"Marketing for Entrepreneurs – Concepts and Application for New Ventures"* Sage Publishing 2022

Economist magazine:

- March 26th 2022, page 59 *"Artificial Prices."*

- November 6th 2021 page 57 "Passing the Buck – Pricing Power."

- October 30th, 2021, page 71 *"Mad Men v. Machine."*

- October 23rd, 2021, page 62 "Why mission statements matter."

- March 13th, 2021, Special Report *"The Retail Renaissance"*.

Eisenmann, Tom. *"Why Start-ups Fail".* Harvard Business Review. May/June 2021 pp77-85.

Fortune magazine:

- November/December 2021, page 28 *"Startups still Vie to be King of the Billboard"*.

- November/December 2021, pp 85 -90 *"Shopping Outside the Aisle"*

- October/November 2021, pp 111 – 124 *"Welcome to the TikTok Economy."*

- August/September 2021. pp F1 -F6. *"World's Largest Companies."*

Hamel, Gary and Zanini, Michele. *"Humanocracy – Creating Organizations as Amazing as the People Inside Them"*, Harvard Business Review Press 2020.

Hanna, Jeannette and Middleton, Alan. *"Ikonica – A Field Guide to Canada's Brandscape"* Douglas & McIntyre 2008

Hood, David James. *"Competitive SME"* Kogan Page Limited 2013.

Knowles, Jonathan. *"Intangible Value is now 85% of the S&P 500."* LinkedIn December 5th 2021.

Knowles, Jonathan. *"Brand Value – 2021 League tables"* LinkedIn October 20th 2021.

Knowles, Jonathan. *"Value-based Brand Measurement and Management"* Interactive Marketing Vol. 5. No.1 pp 40-50. July/September 2003

Kotler, Philip. Kurtajaya, H. and Setiawan, I. *"Marketing 4.0 Moving from Traditional to Digital."* Wiley 2016.

Leger J.L. Nantel J. Duhamel P. Bourque C. and Leger P. *"Cracking the Quebec Code in 45 Minutes."* Les Editions L'Homme" 2022

Leger Reputation Study 2022.

Middleton, Alan C. *"Mentorship Matters – Now More than Ever"* American Marketing Association Toronto Chapter 2021.

Moorman, C. and Lemon, K *"CX RX: Innovating and Competing on Customer Experience"*. Marketing News Summer 2020 pages 46-53.

Parasuraman, A. Zeithamel, V. and Berry, I. *"A Conceptual Model of Service Quality"* Journal of Marketing 49. 1985 ppp 41 – 50.

Romaniuk J. and Sharp B. *"How Brands Grow – Part 2"* Oxford University Press 2022.

Spotlight section of Harvard Business Review *"Why Aren't You Getting More from Your Marketing AI."* July/August 2021 pp 49-59.

Strategy – online newsletter:

- October 25th, 2021 *"Product sampling is one of the best ways to drive trust"*

- August 27th, 2021, *Marketers still struggling to measure ROI"*.

ABOUT THE AUTHOR: ALAN C. MIDDLETON PHD

"We know what we are, but know not what we may become."

From "Hamlet", Act 4, Scene 5, Ophelia. William Shakespeare, 1564-1616, English, playwright, poet, actor.

Alan's 25-year practitioner career includes marketing roles with the Universal Oil Products Company (UOP Inc.) in Chicago, USA; Esso Petroleum in Oslo, Norway; President and 33% owner of Amca Marketing in Toronto, a marketing consultancy; and a career in advertising with the J. Walter Thompson (JWT) advertising agency in the UK, Canada and Japan concluding as President/CEO of JWT Japan and Executive Vice President and a Board Director of the worldwide company.

His 28-year academic career includes teaching at the Rutgers Graduate School of Business in the US, leading business schools in Argentina, China, India, Russia, and Thailand, and from 1998 - 2020, the marketing faculty at the Schulich School of Business, York University where he concluded as Distinguished Adjunct Professor of Marketing. From 2001-2020 he was also Executive Director of the Schulich Executive Education Centre (SEEC) which ran non-degree programs for over 10,000 executives and managers a year domestically and internationally. SEEC was continuously ranked in the top 45 executive and management training organizations in the world.

Alan authored the book *"Mentorship Matters – Now More than Ever"* for AMA Toronto in 2021, and co-authored the books *"Advertising Works II"*, and *"Ikonica – A Fieldguide to Canada's Brandscape"*. He has numerous papers and book chapters published.

He teaches strategy and marketing for entrepreneurs for the York Entrepreneurship Development Institute (YEDI). He sits on Not-For-Profit Boards and Board Committees. These include being an Advisory Board member of AMA Toronto and its Mentor Exchange; Board and Board Committee members of CanadaHelps.org; ABC Life Literacy; Destination Ontario Marketing Metrics Committee; Sunnybrook Health Centre Marketing Committee; Leger Marketing Academic Committee, and others.

He is a co-founder of the 'Cassie' advertising awards, was voted on to the AMA Toronto Canada's Marketing Hall of Legends in the Mentor category in 2005; is a holder of the ACA Gold Medal for contribution to the marketing industry, the Queen Elizabeth II Diamond Jubilee Medal for service to the literacy movement, and the International Association of Business Communicators Toronto Communicator of the Year award.